Crazy Touch

How to be at home with Jesus

Lindsey Hulstrom

WESTBOW
PRESS®
A DIVISION OF THOMAS NELSON
& ZONDERVAN

Scripture quotations taken from the New American Standard Bible® (NASB),
Copyright © 1960, 1962, 1963, 1968, 1971, 1972, 1973, 1975, 1977, 1995
by The Lockman Foundation. Used by permission. www.Lockman.org.

WestBow Press books may be ordered through booksellers or by contacting:

WestBow Press
A Division of Thomas Nelson & Zondervan
1663 Liberty Drive
Bloomington, IN 47403
www.westbowpress.com
1 (866) 928-1240

Because of the dynamic nature of the Internet, any web addresses or
links contained in this book may have changed since publication and
may no longer be valid. The views expressed in this work are solely those
of the author and do not necessarily reflect the views of the publisher,
and the publisher hereby disclaims any responsibility for them.

Any people depicted in stock imagery provided by Thinkstock are models,
and such images are being used for illustrative purposes only.
Certain stock imagery © Thinkstock.

ISBN: 978-1-9736-0398-6 (sc)
ISBN: 978-1-9736-0399-3 (hc)
ISBN: 978-1-9736-0400-6 (e)

Library of Congress Control Number: 2017915370

Print information available on the last page.

WestBow Press rev. date: 01/12/2018

For Daniel,
the one who catches foxes with me

For Nick,
the apple of my eye

So he went away and began to tell...how much Jesus had done for him. Mark 5:18-20

Contents

Foreword

by Susan Brockmann

Lindsey is an answer to prayer. Several years ago I began praying that I would meet faithful Christian girlfriends. It is no chance that Lindsey came into my life.

At church, I had frequently heard her name mentioned among our circle of friends since she was our church secretary. We were still new, and I hadn't had the opportunity to meet this lovely woman about whom I had heard so much.

I began to notice that Lindsey and I attended the same Bible study on Sunday mornings, giving me my first exposure to her insight and eloquence. She would comment on our leader's inquiries with depth and thoughtfulness. I was intrigued. A short time later, we attended a ladies Bible study together where our friendship blossomed.

My circle of comfort is in the realm of writing, rather than speaking. Lindsey can do both, and she does both exceptionally well. She can put into words what I am sensing, feeling, thinking and perceiving.

When she speaks, I say, "Yes, that's right and true and beautiful." Her writing affirms my heart. She has a way of articulating the deepest thoughts and emotions in the most accurate way.

When you read the following pages you, too, will get to know The Lovely Lindsey, as I affectionately call her. Her words speak the truth and always point to Jesus. She shares her struggles, the challenges of motherhood, daily life, and relationships. She reveals her insecurities, but most importantly, her faithfulness. She trusts her Savior because He is our Rock and High Tower. By her example, you'll see how to follow Him when in despair or at the height of joy, and to praise Him through it all.

How blessed I have been to call Lindsey my friend. After you read her words, you will know your Savior more deeply, how she follows Christ, and how she seeks His wisdom. Her strength comes from Him. Her faithfulness will be an example to you, an example to follow to see and know Christ as our only hope and strength.

I am certain you will enjoy getting to know The Lovely Lindsey as much as I have.

First Things First –
The Introduction

We hunger for more than blood to fill our hearts. In our weary-filled world, wouldn't it be great to start and end each day with a heart full of deep meaning, true hope, lasting joy and genuine love?

There is helpful book designed to fill your tank. <u>Crazy Touch</u> captures the longings of our souls, draws you into purposeful dialog with our Creator and provides honest answers during any season. Through short and sweet devotions, this book will encourage people who need comfort, assurance and strength.

As a seasoned veteran in spiritual battles, I've trusted Christ for over 30 years in every kind of terrain. My faith tested in mountains and valleys, I wholeheartedly testify that Jesus is worthy of trust, service and love. He proves Himself the best, most honest companion you can find anywhere!

Believers in all stages of growth crave satisfaction in relating to God and others, and they can have it through the devotions offered in <u>Crazy Touch</u>. Fellow pilgrim, Susan, shares, "Lindsey's words speak the truth and always point to Jesus. She shares her struggles, the challenges of motherhood, daily life, and relationships. She reveals her insecurities, but most importantly, her faithfulness. She trusts her Savior because He is our Rock and High Tower. By her example, you'll see how to follow Him when in despair or at the height of joy, and to praise Him through it all."

I promise that as you pour out your heart honestly to Jesus in everything, *you* will feel His crazy touch. You will experience what it means to grow in His image in awesome ways. You will feel less loneliness. You will have lasting joy. You will have love even for your enemies. You will have hope to face whatever difficulty comes your way, either through your own mistake or the mistake of someone else.

Faith, hope and love are action oriented! Jesus calls you to act as you wait on Him. Don't miss out on what He has for you and how He longs to make your life beautiful. Don't go to bed tonight without sharing all your thoughts, anxieties, mistakes and laughter with Him. Don't wake up tomorrow with an empty heart wondering how in the world I'll make it another day. Don't go through your day without bringing Jesus with you into every eventuality. Your life was not created to be lived without hope, meaning and companionship.

The insights you're going to read are solid ways to relate to God meaningfully, honestly and transparently.

Let Him touch you, then you will touch others and lead them home to Jesus.

A Picture on a Fridge

Being a guest in someone's home is a treat. Not only because you get a literal treat, but because your host is allowing you a more intimate look into their world. One of my favorite places to learn about anyone is from their refrigerator. Not because of what's inside, but what's on the outside.

I especially enjoy a fridge door freckled with many magnets. I love to peruse what's behind the magnets: grocery lists, old doctor appointment reminder cards, a child's masterpiece saying "i luv u mommy," invitations, and my personal favorite - the lopsided Christmas photo greeting card.

I remember getting a Christmas card from old friends when my son was five. They had included a wedding photo of their beaming daughter with her equally beaming new husband. They looked satisfied and content as they proudly posed as newlyweds. I knew next to nothing about this young man, but he meant the world to the young lady at his side whose heart he had stolen.

As I stared at this excited couple, I realized that in a few decades, some stranger would be staring at a photo of my son as a new husband as she opened up her Christmas card. She may think, "Oh how lovely. My friend's daughter got married this year. And boy, did she do well! Their babies are going to be beautiful." Or she may yawn and say "Ho hum, just another card…" Then my son's photo will get put behind a magnet on her fridge door for a bunch of other strangers to see. What that snapshot will hold is more than just an image of some nameless man, and it couldn't begin to share how dear he is to the woman whose heart he first captured, his mom.

His snapshot wouldn't be able to tell that he used to cheer me up when I was pregnant and feeling sad (he really would nudge me from the inside whenever I cried, and it made me smile all over). His picture couldn't tell that when he was 18 months old, he got my slippers for me without asking. His picture won't echo the roars of laughter that kept us sane when we looked together at silly greeting cards at Walmart. Or capture the steady warmth of his soft baby breath in my ear when I cuddled him to sleep. Or reveal how I found myself comforted in the ways that I could comfort him and predict his needs. Or actualize the mutually satisfying companionship we are blessed to share. Or savor the drive thru trips at Culvers to get the flavor of the day custard.

His motionless pose won't reveal to a stranger all the important breakthrough conversations we had when he began to open up about how his parents' divorce affected him. His confident smile won't reveal all his emotional and mental scars or his heart of gold that is full of tenderness, courage, resiliency and forgiveness.

When we look at our old photos together, my son tells me he doesn't remember many of the events I felt were worthy of capturing with my camera. But that's ok. Even though they aren't stored in his memory, I know they are stored in his heart because love wove itself in all those precious times we had together and helped shape him to become the excellent man who will someday share his heart with his beautiful bride.

Together, their lopsided Christmas photo greeting cards may just melt the hearts of hungry guests devouring refrigerator doors.

Barometer Check

I love to read. When I finish a really good book, I feel sad. It's like I'm saying goodbye to a dear friend. I also feel sad because I realize our house is a little messier, and I need to start doing my chores regularly again.

But when I read a book that challenges me to grow in my relationships, especially in my relationship with Christ, I can get really uncomfortable. Not because my house gets messier than usual, but because I realize what a mess I am without the Lord.

These spiritual barometer checks used to overwhelm me. I felt like a spiritual misfit. I felt like I could never be the kind of person I felt God wanted me to be.

I felt my "spiritual to do list" was never ending. In what should have been encouragement, the enemy used well-meaning Christian authors' words to hurl insult after insult in my mind.

Don't get me wrong...I still love absorbing myself in seasoned Christian authors' books to gain spiritual insight. Among my favorites are Anne Graham Lotz, Sylvia Gunter, R.T. Kendall, Gary Smalley, Rosaria Butterfield, Charles Stanley, Francis Chan, Shirley Elliott, and Christine Wyrtzen.

But I've thankfully learned to cherish God's Word first and foremost and find my ultimate security in the promises of the Lord Jesus Christ.

So during any spring cleaning season, I plan on re-organizing my pantry and changing around a few shelves in my kitchen, but I also plan on taking an inventory of what God has already accomplished for me through Christ and how He continues to change my life for the best.

Why don't you take a few moments to find those Bible verses that God uses to speak special meaning into your heart and thank Him for cleansing you through the blood of Christ?

Be A Barnabas

"He was a good man, full of the Holy
Spirit and faith…" Acts 11:24

I hope Barnabas is my neighbor in Heaven. He seems like the kind of guy who would offer to mow my grass if it got too high. Or he'd come by with his own snowplow to clear my driveway. Or he'd greet me with a big smile and listen attentively when I answer his question about how I'm doing.

Barnabas, a.k.a. Son of Encouragement had a most impressive Christian resume! Check it out. He was:
- Generous
- Submissive
- Respectful
- Kind
- Godly
- Bold
- Gentle
- Articulate
- Devoted companion
- Defender of the weak
- Effective advocate
- Christ worshipper

Don't you want him for your neighbor, too?

There aren't any books in the Bible written by Barnabas, but his pupil wrote most of the New Testament. There aren't any famous mega-churches named after Barnabas, but his wonderful generosity provided for the very first church.

Scripture doesn't record his impressive life story. But he gladly gave his life to the One who laid down His life so that all may live. He constantly pursued and defended the unlovable underdog. He was a hero to the unlikely hero. He graciously stayed behind the scenes and gave the spotlight to others. He stayed securely in step with the Holy Spirit when precious relationships took separate paths. He knew that where much had been given, much would be required. He knew where to find grace and mercy in time of need because the grace and mercy of Christ were freely given to him.

Barnabas wasn't perfect, but he pointed people to the only perfect One.

Could it be that Barnabas knew the pain of being unloved and marginalized? Is that what motivated him to love with abandon? Who was it that anonymously loved him into the kingdom?

Who is it that God is calling you to love into the kingdom? Ask Him with great expectation. He already knows them by name because He loves them very much and wants them to become a Barnabas like you and me.

Dear Father, Your Spirit alone made Barnabas a lovable person. He was challenged to build up people when others could not. How lovely are the feet of those who bring good news to set the captives free! Oh, Lord, that our churches would be overflowing with Barnabases! Please make me one of them. In Jesus' Name, Amen.

Becoming Emptied like Jesus

The following is a devotion I shared with my team when my family and I served with e3 Partners in Ecuador during the summer of 2012 on a medical missions trip:

When our team leader told us we couldn't put toilet paper in the toilet, I thought that stunk.

What I didn't realize then was how truly stinky things are around here – the trash, the dirt, the living conditions.

Two days after our arrival in Ambato, I needed an attitude adjustment about how gross I thought stuff was.

The Lord gave me **Philippians 2** in response to my grumblings, and I'd like to use that for our devo this morning.

It says that Jesus emptied Himself. He emptied Himself of his royalty. He left his ultraclean environment of Heaven to become one of us – because He loved us, because He knew we needed Him and to share His message of grace.

Like Jesus, we left behind our comforts of home. We left behind familiar comforts like clean streets, timeliness, traffic laws, and flushing toilet paper down the toilet as often as we wanted.

Jesus also took on the nature of a servant. He said it is better to give than to receive, and He demonstrated that over and over.

One of my favorite examples is in **Matthew 14**. His best friend had been beheaded. Jesus wants to be alone. Instead of taking deserved time to grieve and pour out his heart to the Father, He ends up feeding 5,000 people who just wouldn't leave Him alone.

We're in a foreign land serving strangers who are starving for love, hope and a faith worth dying for. We are helping the sick, adjusting to people and circumstances that are tough. We're making ourselves available to others when we might prefer to be alone.

The last part of Phillippians 2 that I wanted to highlight is verse 8. Jesus humbled himself and became obedient to the point of death. While Jesus' ultimate act of obedience was supremely unique, this passage suggests that Jesus experienced growth as he became obedient.

We are growing in obedience, too. As I thought about this verse, I was quieted by the understanding that I don't think God expects our obedience to be complete overnight.

He sympathizes with our weaknesses and understands that we are frail. He knows the obstacles and temptations we face. He knows about the circumstances and people who test us. He knows our strengths and gifts. Our God is patient with us as we become obedient like Jesus.

The acts of Jesus are awesome, inspiring, convicting and deeply moving. While we don't love, serve, and obey to the same degree as our Lord, I think God understands we still want to be like Christ. He knows we need to be told that He will be faithful to complete the good work He began in us.

In closing, I'd like to encourage you to press on knowing that we happy few are sharing in His sufferings by emptying ourselves, being servants and becoming obedient. Just like Jesus.

Changed for the Better

The following is a speech I made at my church for Sanctity of Life Sunday 2011

I have a confession to make. I get mad about dumb things. I get mad when I'm stuck behind someone on the road when I'm running late. I get mad when my printer at home doesn't print fast. I get mad when I'm running dozens of errands, then my gas light comes on. And honestly, sometimes I get mad when God changes my plans.

Some of us were here last year when we recognized Sanctity of Life Sunday. I remember sitting in the pew feeling glad for the recognition, but I also felt uncomfortable because I couldn't remember the last time I'd prayed about abortion or done something about it. But this past year, things changed.

I read a book called <u>Unplanned</u> by Abby Johnson. I could hardly put it down. It's the transparent autobiography of a former Planned Parenthood director who got saved then started an organization called And Then There Were None. Abby works tirelessly to bring workers out of the abortion industry and into wholeness.

I was deeply moved by Abby's testimony of coming to Christ. But I was also moved by the testimony of the numerous Christians who witnessed to Abby outside her abortion clinic for years. As she noticed their faithful praying, she was softened as they reached out to her in love. She could not shake their unyielding convictions. In her book, Abby mentioned an organization called 40 Days for Life.

I grew more curious about 40 Days for Life. It was started by a small group of Christians who were fed up with the abortion industry and that a generation of Americans grew up under legalized abortion.

So they prayed for one hour seeking the Lord's direction. As they drew near to Him, He drew near to them. God gave them a plan to begin prayer and fasting campaigns that would last 40 days.

The plan involved 40 days of prayer, fasting, and constant vigil outside abortion clinics. The mandate seemed overwhelming, but God is faithful. I'd encourage you to visit their website to learn how God is at work and how you can get involved – it's awesome. It's 40daysforlife.com.

Like I said, I don't always welcome change, but God changed my heart and how I spent some of my time this past year. I prayed with strangers on the sidewalks of Milwaukee and Madison outside abortion mills. My husband and I spent a Saturday evening praying outside a clinic in Madison. I've taken my son with me a couple times on Saturday afternoons to abortion mills, and at the end of our hour, he says, "Wow, that went by fast!" Between the two of us, we've knitted some 100 baby hats for pregnancy care centers. I also went to a small church in West Allis to get sidewalk counseling training.

I receive emails from the 40 days vigil coordinators for Milwaukee and Madison. Dan Miller used to coordinate the Milwaukee outreach. Through Dan's ministry, God saved hundreds of babies and their moms. And you were instrumental in two of those saves.

During one spring campaign, Dan emailed a request for food donations for a lady named Carol who was broke and planned to have an abortion. I oversee the pantry here at church and noticed your donations were coming in, but at that time the needs were low for some reason. When I read Dan's request, I knew why – God had been saving up for Carol. My son and I delivered about six bags of groceries to Dan which he gave to Carol. Her heart grew softer as she listened when Dan told her she and her baby mattered to God.

Carol chose to keep her baby, and she even brought a pregnant friend to meet Dan a few days later. This lady also chose to keep her baby.

It shouldn't surprise me that God still works the same way He did when He fed 5,000 people with a few fish and pieces of bread.

Thankfully, the Lord keeps reminding me to not get mad over dumb things, but at such a time as this, I'm glad He moved me to care about something that's worth changing.

Compensation

Christ redeemed us...having become a
curse for us - for it is written, "Cursed
is everyone who hangs on a tree."
~ Galatians 3:13

For I delivered to you as of first importance
what I also received, that Christ died for our
sins according to the Scriptures, and that He
was buried, and that He was raised on the
third day according to the Scriptures.
~ 1 Corinthians 15:3-4

"If there's a God, then why is there evil?"

"If God is good, then why is there so much evil?"

These are honest, good questions. To be candid, I don't know why God allows evil. If it were up to me, I would erase evil. If it were up to me, I wouldn't allow children to be sold as sex slaves in Cambodia. If it were up to me, I would end abortion. I wouldn't allow married people to commit adultery. I wouldn't allow friendships to fall apart. I wouldn't allow children to be mistreated by their parents. If it were up to me, I wouldn't allow people to be tortured in North Korean labor camps for being Christian.

But it's not up to me. And that's a very good thing because I lack sufficient understanding to rule the universe. It can be so hard to understand why God allows suffering, especially when you are really suffering.

Then it just hurts even more when God in His power chooses not to change circumstances, even when circumstances seem worth changing for good.

Bear with me. Offering intellectual reasons for evil and suffering isn't meant to diminish frustration or anger in suffering. But when the harsh season of loss is eased, consideration of accepting (even embracing) suffering can be made.

It is my sincere hope and prayer for you that you will accept suffering as a refining tool, rather than an instrument of resistance. Coming to this realization is like crossing a spiritual Rubicon. It is empowering.

In his book, <u>God, Freedom and Evil,</u> philosopher Alvin Plantinga says that God creates a world that allows evil and that God has a good reason for allowing it. C.S. Lewis in <u>A Grief Observed</u> said that pain shatters illusions: "Pain insists upon being attended to. God whispers to us in our pleasures, speaks in our consciences, but shouts in our pains. It is his megaphone to rouse a deaf world."

Suffering is as common as breathing, and each of us must inevitably experience trials. But I believe the question for each of us in our suffering is, "What next?" What do we do with suffering - do we embrace it? Despise it? Lash out at the world in response? I don't pretend to have all the answers. I don't say "bring it" for trials just so growth can happen.

But I can say with confidence and through experience that when I yield to God in adversity and obey Him in the seasons of suffering, He brings sweet compensation, reassurance and renewed hope. His truths become clearer, His presence becomes closer and His love for me is more deeply appreciated.

A dear friend of mine told me that I was God's gift of compensation to her. Initially, I felt a little offended. I wasn't her first choice, but in light of being a welcomed substitute for the affection of her estranged adult children, I felt honored to be used by God. I became a source of comfort, companionship, and answer to prayer when her first longing was not actualized.

In one sense, the Bible is story after story of compensation. **Joel 2:25 explains, "The LORD says, 'I will give you back what you lost to the swarming locusts, the hopping locusts, the stripping locusts, and the cutting locusts. It was I who sent this great destroying army against you.'"**

Job 13:15 says, "God might kill me, but I have no other hope. I am going to argue my case with him." What is interesting about this is that God is the one responsible for the loss. He is sovereign, and there is great comfort in a holy God being in control.

Also interesting is that God gives back. We do not deserve anything, let alone the right to ask God for anything. But in His mercy and good will, He gives, takes away and welcomes our questions. Read their stories and observe the lives of others who have accepted God's tool of suffering.

You will see new gravity to their personality that is sweet, like steel frames wrapped in velvet.

Minimizing personal tragedy is a tragedy in and of itself, and believe me, that's the last thing I want to do. Sometimes I feel people can sadly minimize others' suffering because they trivialize it with trite sounding platitudes that only exacerbate the victim's unhealed emotional wound.

There are so many things I love about the Scriptures. One of them is how God addresses the wake emotional suffering leaves behind.

God never trivializes suffering.

He understands that there are times when we do not want words, but instead simply need someone to actualize our own suffering. One of my favorite verses is **Zephaniah 3:17: "For the LORD your God is living among you. He is a mighty savior. He will take delight in you with gladness. With His love, He will calm all your fears. He will rejoice over you with joyful songs."**

He also gives advice to encourage the suffering in **Romans 12:15: "Be happy with those who are happy, and weep with those who weep."**

I find Christianity to be the most satisfying and complete religion in the world. The God of the Bible Himself takes care of evil by paying the price for it all. He doesn't ignore the heinous things people do, but finds those things even more intolerable than we do.

His death on the cross was horrifyingly and beautifully sufficient. The cross screams out from the depths of God's holy heart, "I must act! I must do something to address evil; I must pay the price. Only My sacrifice is worthy to pay it all."

It is so offensive to minimize the deity of Jesus Christ. He is God, and only God could have adequately paid the price for the sin of humanity. The cross screams out His love.

He loves too much to leave us in sin: **John 3:16 says: "For God loved the world so much that he gave his one and only Son, so that everyone who believes in him will not perish but have eternal life."** When you realize how depraved and sick you really are, you can't help but understand that **God is love (1 John 4:8).** Realizing how embarrassingly acquainted He is with my sin causes me to be in awe that He still loves me. He still calls me His bride, His child, His love.

Lord, I love You. Thank You for giving my heart a home. Sometimes I feel suspended in emptiness when I suffer. Even though I may not be satisfied in my circumstances, help me always be satisfied in You.

Crack in Time

I remember the urgency of my mom's voice when she called the morning of September 11, 2001. Just having started maternity leave and happily waiting for the birth of my first child, I was relishing my new morning routine of not having to rush to get to work on time. I got out of bed leisurely and had not even considered opening the outside world to my highly anticipated, sweetly enveloping, Hobbit-like existence.

Like Gandalf's call to Bilbo Baggins to leave the serenity of the Shire, my mom's jolting call shattered my uncomplicated plans of the day. Her frantic tone shot adrenaline through my calm mind, and when I turned on the TV at her urging, the adrenaline turned to dread.

That day in our nation's history was aptly described by Condoleezza Rice as a "crack in time." Destruction was unleashed, and the world as we knew it would never be the same. We groped for answers in a haze of disorientation, and incredulity. How could this have happened? How did we miss the signs? Our impenetrability wasn't just lacerated, it was obliterated. Its wake left behind a sea of destruction that had tsunami-like chain reactions. The domino effects of that day were yet to be fully realized, and the aching void was just beginning to unravel.

A crack in time is a raw epic moment that strips away security and identity. It leaves us in a vigil of bewildering self-preservation management that challenges to the core. It catapults to the unknown and unwanted. It shatters because we know that life will not be the same – it is a severe loss that forces unwelcomed acceptance of punched-in-the-gut change.

We are rudely awakened to the fact that things are not the way they ought to be. We cannot contain the "ought not-ness," and we can't grasp the full picture of its consequence; we just know something really big, something really scary and something way beyond ourselves is unraveling, but we inexplicably want to contain it.

We desperately need to hold onto something bigger and better. And, I believe, we desperately need to know that *that* something worth clinging to is clinging to us in the life-altering process. The nightmare of a crack in time weaves itself into the fabric of our being. Were it not for the handiwork of the Lord, such nightmares would consume us.

His moment by moment, intentional presence is the strong warm blanket that not only covers us. It is the never ending thread that holds us, comforts us and sustains us.

Without minimizing deep felt loss and all platitudes aside, only Jesus Christ is big enough to hold. Only Jesus can grasp the depth of any loss. Only Jesus can make things better. Only Jesus can help ease the sting of searing loss and help us see things differently.

What is your crack in time? Let Jesus speak to you about it.

Be brutally honest with Him about how it hurts. How it frustrates you. How its ripple effect wasn't wanted or nurtured. How it makes you angry.

But don't let your lonely, mad state consume you.

While you pour out your heart to Him, recognize the sweetness He brings. No matter how small it may be, acknowledge any good thing as from Him and thank Him for it.

Trust that His commands are not burdensome. Along the way, as you yield to Him even in painful loss, His companionship will feel even sweeter.

Walking with Him and being known by Him will take on a

different dimension. Your crack in time can be an opening to bring a power at work within you that is far beyond anything you've imagined. His power can help you start to dream again.

Dear Jesus, I got punched in the gut. It hurts so bad I can hardly put it into words. I don't think that this is supposed to happen because it feels so awful. I am beside myself with anger, anxiety, and fear. Please take my anxiety and give me assurance that You know what is happening and that You are mighty to save as Your Word says. Please help me see Your sweet blessings more clearly and help me feel Your presence in a special way. Right now, Lord. Please help me in my unbelief so I see nightmares as a path to trusting You more deeply and so that I can dream again. Please weave my trials into glory for Your kingdom and Your Name. Please help me feel you every millisecond of this day because I feel like I'm going to be swallowed up at any moment. Amen.

Culture Shock

"I will make rivers flow on barren heights, and springs within the valleys. I will turn the desert into pools of water, and the parched ground into springs."
~ Isaiah 41:18

I was introduced to the term "first world problem" during a weekend trip with a few friends at the end of a long Wisconsin winter.

"I just got a new curling iron," I lamented with them, "and it doesn't feel like my old one. I miss it." My friend, Susan, laughed and said, "That is such a first world problem!" How true.

The most rustic part of our weekend was lounging in a cozy four-season porch wrapped in wool blankets gazing at a picturesque scene of a thawing lake. We didn't have to walk miles for water, sleep under a mosquito net or catch dinner as it hopped through the backyard.

As I further ruminated on other pesky "first world problems" I encounter on a daily basis, I realized that I am also a product of being a "first world Christian." I have it easy as a believer in America. I didn't understand how luxurious (or tragic, depending on your perspective) my first world faith experience was until I had a culture shock of the best kind.

I am a child of my age growing up in the 70s and 80s. I sang "School House Rock" jingles when they aired for the first time during Saturday morning cartoons. I knew every Partridge, Brady, Walton, Ewing and Ingalls family member. And when the very first

"Star Wars" movie was released, my family waited in line to buy tickets. Likewise, I am also a child of my Christian culture.

An evangelical of evangelicals, I got saved when a Campus Crusade for Christ missionary shared "The Four Spiritual Laws" tract. I was baptized in a heated swimming pool at the University of Idaho. I've been on many fun church retreats, did a Crusade summer missions project in Hawaii, wore out my 1980s Amy Grant and Michael W. Smith cassettes, enjoyed numerous Bible studies, am well versed in the who's who in evangelicalism, went to Ecuador on a short-term mission trip, prayed outside abortion mills, and even served as my church's office secretary.

In spite of all this engaging activity, nothing quite prepared me for the jolt I got when I was introduced to some eye-opening books and experiences that lead me to wonder if the culture that enveloped me might be quenching the Holy Spirit.

Don't get me wrong; I am so very thankful for the Lord leading a Cru missionary to clearly communicate the Gospel, then baptize me. I was gladly removed from my comfort zone when I shared the Gospel with people in Hawaii and Ecuador. Singing along with Amy Grant and Michael W. Smith was so much better than singing along with my former favorite bands in high school like Van Halen and AC/DC.

I have loved loved *loved* being in Bible studies, praying with like-minded saints, going on retreats and serving alongside people who love and fear God. As I take inventory of all that God has allowed me to touch, I am overwhelmed.

And I feel very, very spoiled.

Find out for yourself in a must-read book, The Heavenly Man: The Remarkable True Story of Chinese Christian Brother Yun. Talk about Christian culture shock!

As I read his biography, I felt like I was getting a spanking and a hug at the same time.

I felt deeply convicted yet encouraged. Brother Yun's biography is nothing short of amazing. It recounts his living as a persecuted believer in China. Brother Yun's discipleship training took place in jail; mine took place on a beach in Honolulu. His wife and her family had to claw their way up jagged cliffs to escape from hounding police simply because of their faith in Christ. I've never been in any physical danger because of my faith.

In short, my experience as a believer in the West does not begin to compare to the experience of believers in harsh countries like China or North Korea.

I sometimes feel guilty for my relative easy experiential Christian culture, but I've also reconciled that my salvation and sanctification are no less valid than someone like Brother Yun. It has nothing to do with him or me or our cultures, but it has everything to do with the object of our mutually cherished faith, the Lord Jesus Christ, and what He accomplished on the cross and in His resurrection for us.

Our growth as Christians will be accomplished through different experiences simply because our Christian cultures are worlds apart, in more ways than one. But the redeeming work of our Creator is just as sweet and important to any of us longing to be more like Jesus.

Aside from the obvious Eastern and Western diametric, any Christian experiences culture shock when we hurt, disappoint and turn against each other. There's nothing quite like being hurt by one of our own, or realizing you are responsible for hurting one of our own.

In spite of such grievances, God continues to be faithful to His beloved bride and so should we. David Brickner of Jews for Jesus summed it up best: "Jesus loves His bride and sees His bride as beautiful and so should we. He is not blind to our flaws or to the reasons for the criticism. He sees those flaws better than anyone because He died to save us from the very sin that makes us such easy targets for rampant criticism. So we need to be careful about harshly criticizing people Jesus loves and died to save."

Following my experience with being shocked by Christians and my culture, God has taught me to be thankful for His work through everything. He has taught me to be gracious to those on the same bumpy journey of sanctification. He has taught me that I desperately need forgiveness more than the person next to me in the pew on Sunday morning.

He has taught me that church can happen anywhere He's invited. He's taught me that His church is bigger than the building we gather in on Sundays. He's taught me that His body is a place where we can experience and be His hands, feet, and heart.

He's taught me that His body is family and that the body sometimes puts the "fun" in "dysfunction!"

He's taught me that His body is a reflection of seasons...a time for silence, a time for speaking up, a time for embracing and a time for space.

His body provides compensation, room to grow and a place where contrasted upbringings don't matter when it comes to giving something beautiful back to the One worshiped together (just ask Jake Luhrs and Matt Greiner of Christian metalcore band, August Burns Red).

He's taught me to welcome contemporary Christian music as it puts my inner angst into words while treasuring old hymns that articulate the numinous truths when my spirit craves reverence.

Keep teaching me to see your people more clearly, Lord!

Days of Elijah and Hagar

Scripture records some of the most exciting accounts in history: Daniel escaping the lion's den, Daniel's friends surviving the fiery furnace, Jonah traveling three days in the belly of a whale, Moses parting the Red Sea, the walls of Jericho falling at the blast of trumpets.

Saturated in the supernatural, these epic stories have captivated kids at bedtime for years and have allowed parents to memorize scripture as they've read them over and over and over. It's easy to detach oneself from biblical jaw-dropping, larger-than-life sagas. As we jump to the chapters that follow such famous accounts, we are drenched in the generous heart of our Heavenly Father.

One of my favorite post-miracle episodes involves Elijah from **1 Kings 18-19**.

Who can forget the awesome defeat of the prophets of Baal when Elijah called fire down from Heaven? Elijah's confrontation with Ahab is reminiscent of David's confrontation with Goliath. Our Old Testament brothers were heroically obstinate in their stance to confront idolatry.

One can not help but cheer on their Yahweh-anchored resoluteness which seemed completely impenetrable. While Elijah's victory was one for the ages, what happens next was even more remarkable.

It seems unbelievable that Elijah would fall apart when he heard that Jezebel planned to kill him after Baal was defeated.

- Who would have guessed that after boldly broadcasting the power of God before hundreds of his enemies, Elijah cowered before just one?
- How could wisdom escape him so quickly?
- Didn't Elijah realize how vulnerable he was making himself by leaving his companion and heading into the desert alone?
- How could this pillar of iron melt like a stick of butter when things got hot?
- Is it really possible Elijah and Jonah were ancestral kindred spirits as they cried to the Lord to let them die in the face of adversity **(Jonah 4:9)**?

Even as Elijah's faith surprisingly wavered, the Lord he had testified about proved Himself closer than a brother.
- While Elijah cried for death to take him, God provided rest and nourishment **(1 Kings 19:6)**
- Where Elijah failed for lack of vision and stamina, God provided direction and strength **(19:8)**
- When Elijah was homeless, God provided shelter **(19:9)**

God graciously provided what Elijah needed before his heart could be receptive to His gentle whisper of admonishment, a renewed assignment, and a new companion.

God wasn't harsh with his servant; He dealt with Elijah ever so gently and reaffirmed the calling Elijah had followed before falling apart. Hallelujah! What a Savior! What a Friend!

Just as there is an ancestral kindred spirit linking Elijah and Jonah, there is also one linking our hero to Hagar.

Like Elijah, Hagar ran into the desert fleeing the wrath of an angry woman **(Genesis 16:6)**. Hagar was alone but was not abandoned, either. She also received the supernatural wake-up call, "What are you doing here?" **(Gen. 16:8, 1 Kings 19:13)**

Not that the Lord needed clarification Himself, but He wanted

His servants to answer the question for themselves. Hagar and Elijah were given the mandate to return from where they ran.

While scripture doesn't tell us their reactions, I wonder if they thought, "Go back?! Are You for real, God?"

But God didn't just rain on their parades.

Instead, He gives new promises and new hope in their seasons of desperation.

For Hagar, it was the same promise He gave to Abraham: descendants too numerous to count. God had a big plan for Abraham, and His plan was no less important for Hagar, just very different.

For Elijah, it was the honor of anointing two kings and anointing his successor, Elisha. God still had much work for Elijah to do, and God gave him a wise, faithful friend to help him accomplish it all.

Just when it seemed like Hagar and Elijah's stories were all dried up, God in His lavish mystical sovereignty, pours out living water to revive and refresh their parched souls to partner with Him in accomplishing His will.

And as they obeyed to do what seemed impossible, the Lord kindly gave them the desires of their hearts.

Father God, You are amazing. What seemed like a death sentence for Hagar and Elijah was life-giving. You gave them what they needed in the desert and what they needed to accomplish Your will. It is a mystery, Lord, to realize their intimate needs were wound up in Your huge plans for the world. As Elijah and Hagar ran away in fear, thank You that You gently called them back to Your big Father heart. Thank You that Your big Father heart is for me, too. Thank You that Your big plans involve me, too. Help me to always run back home to You. You are my hiding place, my shelter, my fortress, my compass, my strength. May our hearts always be at home with each other. In Jesus' Name, Amen.

Dead on Arrival

My life began when I died.

And whenever I think I've finally arrived in life, then I know it's time to die again to myself so that I can live again.

I was 18 when I understood that I needed to get busy living. I was a freshman in college and was invited to consider how I related to God.

I thought we got along well enough; after all, exercising a vague belief in God seemed like it wasn't hurting anyone, let alone Him. I didn't know it at the time, but my relationship with God was dead because I was suffocating the life He longed to breathe into my parched life. He created me, loved me, provided for me, and was taking very good care of me.

I was tragically oblivious to the depth of His goodness and was sadly guarding myself against His wonderful touch. Let me share how our relationship got started on the right foot.

Christ died on a cross for my sins according to the Scriptures. He was buried then raised on the third day according to the Scriptures. God loved me so much that He sent His one and only Son to die for me so that I can have eternal life. God is not like you and me; He is holy and almighty. He was, He is, and He is to come. I have sinned against Him so deeply and so offensively that I deserve death. But He cares for me so much that even while I nurtured enmity against Him, He laid down His life to spare me from death.

But it's not just enough to know these things. Just as God

acted for me, I need to act toward Him. Believing in the Lord and accepting His payment for sin saves. Without God's perfect payment for sin and my receiving His gracious gift, I am bankrupt in spiritual debt with absolutely no hope of reaching any adequate settlement. His awesome love has arrived in His Son, Jesus, and I'd rather be in His grip than in anyone else's. Won't you nurture His friendship by receiving Jesus now? He longs to be gracious to you!

This cosmic reconciliation is worth getting excited about! Now, I'm not a verbose savant like authors Eric Metaxas or Victor Hugo, but I am so excited to share with you in the following pages how Christ has touched me.

His work gloriously undoes what I've become, and I am so thrilled to be known by Him. He teaches me to see His hand behind the scenes of imperfect human events.

By His grace, I can accept the realities of life and still see the sun behind clouds.

I've learned that even though the night has a thousand eyes, His gentle eye shines brighter and never stops gazing on me in love.

I've learned that His intense honesty and sacrificial goodness infuses me with lasting hope and joy.

I've learned that God is big enough to hold the universe in His hand yet is intimately close for me to pray about something as small and childlike as my pet hamster.

I've learned that walking with Christ makes it a lot easier talking about stampeding elephants from every corner of life.

Most of all, I've learned that living for Christ alone gives me something worth dying for.

Cry out to the Lord to start living. You won't want to let go of His touch.

Faith Works

The following is a speech I gave at my church to share about my involvement in one of our outreaches.

I don't know about you, but my ideal Sunday is to have an excellent time at church, hear a good sermon, visit with friends, then go home, take a nap and eat brownies. But not necessarily in that order. The last thing that's on my mind is to spend my day off going door to door talking with dozens of strangers.

But a few years ago, I felt compelled to get out of my comfortable Sunday routine to do just that.

Our Bible study leaders gently encourage us to always look for ways to be challenged in our walk with the Lord. Faith Works was a new ministry for my church when I was asked to canvass neighborhoods to let folks know about our service.

In the fall of 2008, I had done some door to door campaigning for the presidential campaign. I had never done anything like that. I was pleasantly surprised to find people were friendly and no one slammed their door on me.

A few months later, when volunteers were needed for canvassing, I thought, if I had sacrificed time to campaign for a president, surely I could be an ambassador for my church. So I prayed for courage and asked God to help me do this. He kindly provided beautiful sunny weather.

I was assigned an area in the north central part of town and went to task. I knocked on about 200 doors during a few Sunday afternoons. Some doors didn't open, and I wonder if people had looked out their windows and thought I was too intimidating (I'm just shy of 5'1").

Those who did open their doors were friendly and gracious. When I explained our church wanted to help with home repairs for free, they were stunned. "Really? No strings?" "Really, we just want to share the love of Christ with our neighbors and show you we care about you." I even got to know some of my church family members better by knocking on their doors, too.

Last year, they asked for canvassers again, and I signed up even though I felt very busy with school and work. Thankfully, I had the pleasure of canvassing with a dear sister in Christ. It was great having someone to walk and pray with in the same neighborhood I'd canvassed the year before.

The Lord opened several doors for us to pray with people and listen to their stories of need – older ladies whose husbands were not well, an elderly couple who didn't get out much and a mom grieving over her wayward child. A few people had remembered me from the previous year and many commented that they'd heard about Faith Works.

Almost everyone seemed relaxed and glad to see us doing the same work again. I'd like to share one story in particular.

We'd knocked on the door of a gentleman, and we introduced ourselves, he had a big grin and said, "You told me about your church last year, and others did work on my house last year! You guys did a great job. You know, when I told a friend what you were doing, he said, 'They'll make you join their church or ask you for money.'" When our crew finished, he went back to his friend and told him he was wrong. The thing about this testimony was how far reaching our seemingly small labors reach others. Here was this man who took us up on this crazy offer to help him with no strings attached. He told his friends and family about it.

They thought for sure we would want something in return. But we didn't.

We simply wanted to demonstrate the kindness of our wonderful Savior in a tangible way. Our approach made an impact on him and his community, and I believe will cause their hearts to melt and be more receptive to the Holy Spirit.

It was my joy and privilege to be an ambassador for our church during those days and to play a small part in the greater plan of helping people see Christ more clearly.

In the Book of Titus, we are told over and over to be eager to do good. Literally stepping out in faith to knock on stranger's doors was intimidating, but I'm confident it was a good work that God was pleased I did.

And I've even been able to enjoy a few naps and brownies since then.

Famous Last Words

"Go therefore and make disciples of all the nations, baptizing the in the name of the Father and the Son and the Holy Spirit, teaching them to observe all that I commanded you; and I am with you always, even to the end of the age." ~ Matthew 28:19-20

My son sometimes talks about the "college countdown" where he tells me how many years are left before he goes off to college. He reminded me of this when I dropped him off at school. As I drove away, I felt a pang in my heart.

I talked with the Lord about how I felt that my only child will need me less as he gets older. I told the Lord that it makes me sad thinking about not being current with Nick or having as much time to make memories with him. I asked Him to help me accept the inevitable with grace and less discomfort. Then I went about my usual time of prayer in the car before I arrived at the office.

As I was lying in bed that night, I thought of what I would say to Nick when I dropped him off at college. Sadly, the first thing that came to my mind was to tell him to not get into trouble.

Within seconds, the final words of Jesus came to mind. I was gripped with the difference between His last words to His children compared to what I imagined my last words might be to my son when he enters his adult world without me.

By contrast, the Lord's famous last words were not laced with "don't be naughty." Instead, His were laced with purpose, infused with hope and confidence in the disciples' ability to succeed, not with chastisement.

I've heard Matthew 28:19-20 probably a thousand times, but I was so glad the Lord gave me a new perspective on it. Christ's final words were not just about disciplining, but they were loaded with faith, hope and love. Jesus had said that unless He left, the Helper wouldn't come **(John 16:7).** If it were up to me, I would not have chosen for Jesus ever to leave. But separation was the Father's plan for His Son and the Holy Spirit in order to build His kingdom most gloriously.

The Lord had answered my prayer from earlier in the day when my son reminded me of his inevitable and much-needed departure from my nest.

I needed comfort from Him to appreciate the imminent separation between my son and me. He showed me through these famous last words that Jesus separated Himself from the disciples, just like Nick and I will separate.

Like the Helper doing His work in the disciples, I need to be removed in certain areas of my son's life for Him to accomplish His will in Nick's life most gloriously.

He also reassured me that He will accomplish what He pleases in my son's life, far better than I ever could imagine. It struck me that God, in what appears to be inopportune times like lying awake at two in the morning, sometimes answers us profoundly.

As I step aside for the Lord to take care of my beloved son, His promise to gently guide those who have young rings true in the deepest parts of my heart **(Isaiah 40:11).**

Father's Love

"...our fellowship is with the Father, and with His Son Jesus Christ...so that you may know that you have eternal life." 1 John 1:3, 5:13

How could you not love David...repentant sinner, driven leader, godly king, poet, musician, prophet, gracious servant, valiant soldier, handsome man, loyal friend, humble, generous, gregarious? Reading David's life in the Old Testament could be like reading a great novel, but when someone is called "a man after God's own heart," you have to wonder how someone earned that kind of honor. He certainly responded in godly ways when confronted with his ugly sin and when he chose not to take the life of Saul.

But I wonder if he was after God's own heart the deepest when he struggled over his son, Absalom.

It's one of the most moving accounts of parental love in all of Scripture: Rebellious Absalom rallies an army to overthrow his father from his throne. Even after David's loyal army suffers heavy casualties to keep him on the throne, the king admonishes his leaders, **"Deal gently for my sake with the young man Absalom." (2 Samuel 18:5)**

Following victory and rather than seeing to the needs of his kingdom, David only longs for his son. Upon hearing news of Absalom's murder, all he can do is weep and mourn. His cries for his son are breathtakingly intimate and moving: **"O my son Absalom,**

my son, my son, Absalom! Would I have died instead of you, O Absalom, my son, my son!"

Then in comes the man of the hour: Joab. His duplicity is unnerving. But were it not for Joab, David may have sunk into a spiraling deep pit of loss upon loss. Joab's demand for his friend to behave like a king not only saves the kingdom, it also reminds us why we love David: holiness.

David was bereft, but it was for righteousness he stepped out of his personal agony to have justice served and to acknowledge the wrong his son had done. Isn't that like the love God the Father demonstrates for us...He weeps over our rotten rebellion, but His holiness demands justice. It's because of God's holiness that we can trust Him, serve Him and love Him as our Abba Father God.

Even though you and I are not eyewitnesses to His glory like John and the other apostles, we who are in Christ have the assurance that we are His very own children. What an utterly magnificent thought!

God in Heaven weeps over our rebellion, but because He longs to be gracious to us and because of His holiness, He died for our sin so we may have fellowship with Him and to know that we have eternal life.

He wants you to know this so that you can tell someone else about your awesome, incomparable Father who loves you like David loved his Absalom.

For Pete's Sake

Who's your favorite apostle? No-nonsense James, shrewd businessman Matthew, doubting Thomas, zealous Simon, shy Andrew, observant John or brash Peter?

Regardless of who you identify with most, each of the men Jesus chose to follow Him was so different from one another it's a wonder they got along! Despite their differences, they agreed on the solid truth of who Jesus is and what He meant to each of them. Just as each apostle grew in the rich knowledge of God's love, so do we who are in Christ.

But unlike the apostles who believed because they had seen, Jesus said of us: **"...blessed are those who have not seen and yet have believed." (John 20:29)**

When Jesus told Peter and Andrew that He would make them fishers of men, He was making a promise. He had big plans for them, and the brothers were exercising tiny faith when they left their fishing nets to follow Him. But that tiny faith was all they needed for the time being **(Matthew 17:20)**.

Their future success wasn't completely on their shoulders. On the contrary, it was up to Christ. **First Thessalonians 5:24 says: "Faithful is He who calls you, and He also will bring it to pass." Deuteronomy 7:9 says, "Know therefore that the LORD your God is God; he is the faithful God."**

Jesus relates to each of His friends uniquely. He wants each person to believe in and experience His love, power, and presence in every eventuality.

He wants to make His home in our hearts so the Holy Spirit can help us fulfill His calling in our lives **(John 15)**. Followers of Christ testify to who He is (the only true, living God), what He accomplished on the cross, that He rose from the dead and that He will judge the world. As they testify to these universal truths, they experience personal witness of Jesus in their lives and observe His activity in the lives of the brethren.

Convinced of His good character, our confidence in the Lord grows, and we can be sure our faith is not in vain.

While I wouldn't identify most with Peter (I feel I identify more with Andrew and a little of John), his life has epic moments every maturing Christian can identify with.

Contrast **Mark 4:38 and Acts 12:6** - in Mark 4:38, Jesus is sleeping during a sea storm while His disciples are freaking out. They can't understand how He can rest during such an unpredictable time. Fast forward to Acts 12:6, and it's now *Peter* who is sound asleep the night before he is scheduled to be executed!

Can it be that the work of Christ in our lives produces such peace, rest, and calmness in the storms of life? There was evidence in Peter's life that it sure does.

- Like Peter, and with the help of the Holy Spirit, we become people of integrity.
- Like Peter, we can invest our lives in people because we begin to care for people like God cares for people.
- Like Peter, we can influence people for Christ's kingdom.
- Like Peter, we can be forgiven and reinstated when we bitterly fail **(John 21:19).**
- Like Peter, we can know that we know we belong to the One who is faithful.

It isn't always easy following Jesus, but it is so worth it. Come and see the Lord is good. Once you understand what He offers, how could you not want Him to make home with you?

Lord Jesus, thank You for being faithful. Thank You for casting vision for each of your children and that Your promise to bring it to pass is trustworthy. Thank You for making Your bride beautiful, not because of anything done on our own, but because of Your greatness. Help us be like Peter, who had childlike faith to sleep while storms raged around him. In Your Name, Amen

Foxy

Catch for us the foxes, the little foxes that ruin the vineyards, our vineyards that are in bloom. ~ Song of Solomon 2:15

Our cat, Purrhana, has delightfully grown on us since he joined our family. He follows us everywhere and makes himself at home on our laps, chairs, beds, windowpanes, and in empty boxes. His playful behavior thankfully gives us moments of levity each day.

While we caught him at the animal shelter years ago, my husband, Daniel, and I have been catching another rascally animal daily - the fox (of sin). While this cunning creature displays his unwelcome presence into our tranquil lives, I can't imagine catching them with anyone else but Daniel.

In some ways, Daniel and I are like peas and carrots.

We like to pun, kayak, eat easy dinners, watch old episodes of "Little House on the Prairie", bike ride, take walks in the neighborhood, talk for hours, camp, applaud frugality, listen attentively to others, exercise kindness and mercy, laugh a lot, visit alpaca farms and discuss the virtues of wool, provide mutual comfort, enjoy quiet and do not let hard knocks keep us down for long.

In other ways, we are like oil and water.

He keeps, I purge. He gets busy on Saturday mornings, I stay in my jammies as long as I can. Daniel thrives on continuity, I thrive on change. Throughout our lifetimes, he's lived in 2 towns, and I've lived in 17. He swims, I run. He drinks tea, I drink coffee. He's never had a cavity, and I've lost count. He's rarely in a hurry, but I've got a lead foot. He's not familiar with music from the 70s and 80s but I can sing along to an old BeeGees or U2 song in a heartbeat. He has skin like a wet duck, while mine absorbs way more than it should.

Our similarities and differences embody **Proverbs 27:17 - "As iron sharpens iron, so one person sharpens another."** Our later-in-life union brings us deep joy as we pray often together and keep our eyes fixed on Jesus, the author and perfecter of our faith and essential cord of **Ecclesiastes 4:12 - "Though one may be overpowered, two can defend themselves. A cord of three strands is not quickly broken."**

I love what Daniel's love does to me.

He believes in me in ways no one ever has. I appreciate his gentleness and approachability. I treasure his faithful companionship. I rely on his patience, steadiness, maturity, insightfulness, helpful feedback, consistent availability, wholesome sense of humor and his cheerful mantra, "Onward and upward!" I am blessed by his servant's heart and that he has a good name. I am warmed when he tucks me in and kisses me goodnight.

I feel relieved when he tells me I'm beautiful after I gaze at my aging frame in the mirror. I breathe easier knowing he is slow to get angry. I am comforted by his strong, smooth hand entwined in mine as we walk in public. I feel like a queen when my knight in shining armor always opens doors for me. I relish being listened to and taken seriously. I get excited hearing the garage door open when Daniel comes home and that we can safely share about our day.

I am grateful we forgive each other and can move quickly toward healing because our love account has so many rich deposits, so many sweet memories, so much trust, so much genuine good will, so much laughter, so many secrets, so many right choices, so much security.

My man catches those little foxes like no one else can, and I respect him deeply. Daniel, I love you and thank God you waited for me.

Great Expectations

Charles Dickens captured Victorian England in his novels. He captured the human condition well in his infamous character from <u>Great Expectations</u>, Miss Haversham.

While it's been years since it was required reading for my ninth grade English class, we all thought Miss Haversham was a bit creepy. She had been jilted at the altar and couldn't seem to get over her pain as she wore her wedding dress until her dying day. The bright gown that once beheld her beauty became a dark cloak of permanent mourning, and its display in public humiliation only compounded her misery.

Miss Haversham expected great things to follow her wedding day: a promise to be loved, to build a life with her beloved, to be protected and to have her identity blended with another who shared her heart, dreams and expectations. Instead, she received a broken heart, shame, loneliness and a shattered future.

Life is wrought with expectation. I believe this stems from being made in God's image. Our Creator is highly active and involved in our daily lives. He doesn't seem to exist merely to be worshiped. He is altogether relationally existent and responsive within the Trinity and with His entire creation.

Indeed, God is yearning for those whose hearts are fully His so He can add to their strength **(2 Chronicles 16:9).** As we live, move and have our being in Him, we anticipate so many things from basic sustenance to lavish vacations.

He allows us to dream big dreams and, sometimes, He graciously gives us our wants in addition to the needs He promises through Christ.

But what if our expectations are good and modest, yet go unfulfilled day after day? Like the cloak that enveloped Miss Haversham, those haunting unmet expectations can unravel the tapestry of faith God longs to knit in the human heart.

Pain demands to be felt, and its wake can leave the victim struggling to find a way to swim in raging waters of seemingly endless despair and hopelessness.

When I was a young believer, I could not read the book of James. I avoided it for years because it made me so uncomfortable.

The idea of rejoicing in trial was like finding delight in putting your hand in a pot of boiling water. But God was patient.

Through the years, He brought me back to James when little trials came my way, like dealing with a difficult co-worker or receiving correction from my boss or when my car got stuck in the snow. Now when I read James, I marvel at how God has truly changed my perspective on suffering.

Jesus promised that in this world we would have trials. This world is tragically fallen and overflowing with sin. Who am I to be immune from its effects?

In its most intense forms, I have found God to be intimately close in times of excruciating loss.

As I read Job one morning in the early stages of being laid off my job as a single mom, I truly understood that God allowed the loss.

If I accepted Him to be good as His Word says, and since I loved Him in pleasant times, why shouldn't I continue loving Him in times of want?

How could I not still love Him just as much since He was the same God who allowed the easy times?

The grasp of His intimate presence in the valley of darkness comforted me with tremendous assurance, and I knew He was right there with me. He had a purpose for changing my comfortable, desired circumstances. While His purpose and goal for me was unknown at that moment, I could rely on His promises to see me through.

The peace that surpassed my understanding has since seen me through many more valleys. While I don't pray for suffering, I do know that yielding to God in times of pain sooner than later makes the journey quicker and even sweeter.

I know He has riches to share in those secret places and during unwanted seasons, and I understand His heart and even His pain better as I take His yoke upon me in trust and in love.

Yieldedness to God in the depth of suffering brings spiritual peace I would not trade for the world.

Father God, Your Word promises that I won't be burned when I walk through the fire. Even in times of agony when I've cried for You to take away my pain or make things different, I have felt Your abiding presence. Take away my expectations of a painless existence so I don't miss more of You. Help me trust in Your all-encompassing, loving presence and power to bring good, no matter my circumstances. Please make Yourself so real to me that I can tell You all about myself and my sorrows. I feel You listening to me with all Your heart, and it feels good. I love You.

Heroes

Who's your hero? I remember my first hero, the Bionic Woman. Lindsay Wagner ran alongside the Six Million Dollar Man with a winning smile, lept onto buildings with ease, and could hear whispers from a mile away. When she effortlessly tore in half a four inch phone book, my six year old frame was glued to the TV in awe of this super woman.

The editor-in-chief of Marvel Comics, Axel Alonso, says, "Kids need heroes. While parents should be role models for life, superheroes remind a child of the moral compass necessary to navigate a universe fraught with thrills and danger." While Alonso may not be a voice for the ages, there is some truth to what he says.

There's a kid in all of us that wants a hero to save the day.

Aren't most of us searching for someone or something bigger than ourselves in which to find delight and security? Heroes help take the sting out of the ordinary stuff of life, and they take care of the monster in the closet.

Those monsters take all kinds of shape: a bully, unrequieted love, a distorted view of oneself, believed lies, a struggling bank account, poor health, pride, fear, insecurity, homelessness… monsters perpetually hound us mentally, emotionally, physically and spiritually. In the midst of such predators, it seems our right to demand heroes.

It's easy to admire larger-than-life historical heroes like George Washington or Abraham Lincoln or Dietrich Bonhoeffer. Or even contemporary heroes like John Piper, Billy Graham or Meriam Yahia (the imprisoned Sudanese woman who had been sentenced to death for refusing to give up her Christian faith). Their established, yet distanced, character is inspiring and challenging. In a way, some distance is preferred because without that, they may become less heroic.

Heroes and perfection go hand in hand. But is it fair to require perfection from heroes, let alone anyone? Of course not, but I do it all the time with everyday people who I read about or who make promises to me or who seem to be in positions to provide what I feel I need or want.

I embrace an image rather than reality. My sin nature can become scarier than any monster in the closet because I exchange an image for the Creator as I look for perfection in others. When I confess putting too much demand on someone, God allows me to experience His grace in sweet measure. When I ask myself who hasn't disappointed or who I haven't disappointed, the answer comes full circle: hope in God.

Psalm 18:30 says, "As for God, his way is perfect: The LORD's word is flawless; he shields all who take refuge in him." Thankfully, **His ways are not our ways (Isaiah 55:8)**. Hoping in the perfect God removes fear **(1 John 4:18).** When I realize my own limitations and imperfections, I run to Him because He is my shield and He restores my soul **(Psalm 23:3)**.

I need to always run to Christ to be my perfect hero because He will always protect, restore and act justly.

Father God, You alone are holy. Your perfection is my delight and my security. Forgive me when I have put my hope in people more than in You. Help me let go of unrealistic expectations of people and free me from the scary monsters that can rob me of intimacy with You. Help me cling to You always for You are my rock and fortress. Thank You for always being there for me and for showering me with your grace and mercy. In Christ's Name. Amen.

His Bride, His Treasure

Ever have one of those times when you think you're driving in the right direction, only to find out the road you need to turn down has a roadblock sign?

It's one of those times that you wished your GPS had ESP (and that you had downloaded the newly available maps from garmin.com to the electronic version of your fancy Rand McNally *before* your trip).

I had one of those times when I was driving home from an evening writing class. Thankfully, I was able to get decent radio reception as I drove through August-high cornfields in southern Wisconsin. I tuned in to a program that I infrequently listen to but found utterly captivating and encouraging.

It was John MacArthur's "Grace to You," and he started it off by unapologetically declaring, "I love the church!" His message centered around the One who loves the church even more, the Lord Jesus Christ. It's a delight listening to a seasoned teacher of the Word who has earned the right to be heard, and I suppose that's what drew me in.

Thankfully, in a round about way and several gallons of gas later, I made it home safe and more sound than when I had left because of the detour God had in store for me that evening.

Hearing someone who's been in ministry for most of his adult life say he STILL loves the church with humility, sincerity and authenticity is compelling, and my heart overflows with thanksgiving for people who are like that.

What is more compelling is that Jesus still loves His church. He sees His church - His bride - as beautiful, even with all her blemishes and fragmentation. His beloved bride is His cherished treasure that He laid down His life to save and to grow into His image. She is utterly precious to Him, and she takes His breath away. She also causes Him untold heartache and grief at times.

Because His blood covers her flaws and infuses her with righteousness, it fills me with joy and compulsion to be part of His team and to keep loving the team. His presence and faithfulness is the heart of the church, and thankfully, in spite of her imperfections, His will always see her as lovely because He is love.

In his splendid book, The Boys in the Boat, Daniel James Brown recounts the revelation champion rower Joe Rantz received from boat maker, George Pocock, who was dispensing wisdom to this young man during a crossroads in his life: "If you don't like some fellow in the boat, Joe, you have to learn to like him. It has to matter to you whether he wins the race, not just whether you do."

Pocock continued to share that it mattered more than how hard a man rowed was how well everything he did in the boat harmonized with what the other fellows were doing. And a man couldn't harmonize with his crew mates unless he opened his heart to them. He had to care about his crew.

It wasn't just the rowing but his crewmates that he had to give himself up to, even if it meant getting his feelings hurt.

- Doesn't this capture **John 15:13** and **1 Corinthians 13** beautifully?
- Doesn't it make you want to be in that kind of boat where differently gifted people are exerting their strength for the good of one another?
- Who share their hearts with one another by caring, by studying, by listening, by shutting up, by speaking up?
- Doesn't this pep talk make you want to obey the church's greatest coxswain, Christ the Lord, as He bellows out encouragement and direction?

Oh, please, please where do I sign up??

When I consider how much I love the Lord and how He means everything to me, I sometimes forget that He loves all His children that much. I lose sight of being part of His large family in His great big boat, and I sadly lose sight of His longing to have His children love another as He loves us.

When I consider what my life would be without the church - warts and all - I feel sad. And so should the world.

The church is God's presence on earth and His barometer of goodness. The church is where God's plan for people to live well and to love more fully comes into fruition.

Wish for more good living and good loving in the church? I do, too! Then please, please pray with me.

Our Father, thank You for loving and saving us. Thank You, Lord, for pouring out Your life for Your church. Thank You for loving Your people and calling them Your very own. Thank You that nothing will ever keep Your people from Your love. In spite of our shortcomings and flaws, You never leave us or forsake us. You refresh us, strengthen us, infuse us with hope and give us joy. Please grant Your church repentance and revival. Please Lord, help me to love Your people as you would have me to. Where I need to come to terms with how undependable and untrustworthy Your people sometimes can be, help me trust in You enough to give them the benefit of the doubt, to let them off the hook and to believe in them like You believe in me. Help me not see others' sin looming so large that I lose sight of my own. Help me to to keep praying for Your bride, Your treasure, and be as generous as possible in giving to Your body in all its many efforts and outreaches. And as I love Your people, and love the people who will be Your people as they enter our fellowships, I long to become more and more like You, my beloved groom, savior and friend. In the name of Jesus, Amen.

Hundred Year Hug

As I feel your big strong arms around my tinier frame, I don't want your hug to end. I want it to last one hundred years. Is that too much to ask?

You can sense when my hurting heart needs no words but needs your soft touch. I want your touch to last one hundred years. Is that too much to ask?

Our empty arms ached for something sweet for what seemed to be one hundred years, and now that we've filled them, I want them to be filled one hundred years. Is that too much to ask?

Your arms are so welcoming, inviting and melting. It takes hundreds of kind little things, following hundreds of days, to feel at home in your tender grip.

Your hugs envelope like a thick, cozy blanket that's just been removed from the dryer.

Your hugs are like rays of rich sunshine on a summer day that splash across my raised, warmed smiling face.

Your hugs are like a strawberry moon - one-of-a-kind, bright, full, well-rounded, signaled, highly-anticipated and captures the harvest of love awakened at the right time.

Your hugs are like coveted morning coffee drenched in cream and sugar in my heavy M.A. Hadley pottery kitty mug.

Your hugs are like a sea of rows and rows of colorful tulips that dance across acres of otherwise bare landscape.

Your hugs are like delicious homemade rich and frothy egg nog with a dash of nutmeg on top.

Your hugs are like the smell of maple sausage and bacon on a leisure Saturday morning in my jammies.

Your hugs are like filling my honda fit gas tank to full when oil prices are low.

Your hugs are the smoothie of the month at Basics Co-op - ever-changing, yet wonderfully familiar.

As much as I feel comforted by your hugs, I sense your guiding arms are just as comforted having someone to have and to hold.

Your hundred year hug feels like home, and I don't want home to end for one hundred years. Is that too much to ask?

I'm Lovin' It

I have to confess something. I've been eating at McDonald's since I was two.

One of my Mom's favorite things to do is to shop. I was her "Shopping Buddy" from the time I was a few months old till I got my first job in high school. Any mother who's taken her toddler shopping knows kids get bored. As soon as I would get fussy, my Mom would get me a little packet of McDonald's french fries. And then we'd be golden just like those famous arches for a few more hours at the mall.

I've been visiting McDonald's less since I joined a friendly Slimdown Challenge, but found myself in one of their booths recently for one of the most memorable times there ever. My son was at his school's activity night on a Friday, and I needed to occupy my time for a few hours.

On a "whim" I thought I'd go to McDonald's and write my blog on spring cleaning. I got cozy, opened the Chromebook and after I'd added some things to our Google calendar, a stranger approached me.

"'Scuse me, but can I ax you somethin'?" I looked up feeling a little surprised and said: "Uh, sure." He said, "I just came up here from Atlanta, and I'm stayin' with family. I'm thinkin' of moving to Wisconsin. What do you like about livin' here?"

Moving to Wisconsin from Athens, Georgia 10 years ago, it was easy for me to compare and share. James seemed eager for conversation. After we talked for about 15 minutes, I felt a nudge from the Holy Spirit, so I asked James if I could pray for him. His face softened, and he said he would like that.

He put his hand out, I took it, then prayed. I thanked the Lord for bringing James to Wisconsin, for his family and that He would help everything work out if it was His will for a move. When I was finished, James earnestly thanked me, then proceeded to tearfully share more about his tough background. I felt honored to listen and to be trusted.

There have been more times than I care to remember where I've passed opportunities to actually share the gospel with someone, but I did not want to pass this chance up with James. I prayed silently, "Lord, help me share Your Word with this man. Help me know how to encourage James in You."

God was gracious, and He opened the door to me to share the good news. I keep a small supply of tracts in my purse, and sadly, they go unused. Not tonight, though. As I shared, James asked thoughtful questions, and I felt the Spirit helping me along. It felt glorious being used to plant seeds in a hungry heart.

Before I knew it, I needed to pick up my son. As we parted company, James asked me to keep praying for him. I told him I certainly would be praying for him.

When I do a spring cleaning inventory of my service to the Lord, evangelism is always an area of weakness. I get tongue-tied, distracted or allow myself to feel intimidated and inadequate.

Can you relate?

I am incredibly thankful to the Lord for moving James to initiate conversation with me that evening. I am thankful God gives us what we need to serve Him and others. I am thankful God let me serve Him by showing compassion and kindness to a lonely stranger at McDonald's. I'm glad God disrupts our plans to fit into His plans. Please pray for James with me... that God will continue to draw him to Himself and that He will protect our new friend from the evil one. Thanks.

Make Me a Naomi

That is not a typo.

We're familiar with the undeniable heroine of the book of Ruth – the poor young woman who loyally stayed by an old woman's side captured the heart of the man of peace of a foreign community, then mothered a direct descendant of the Messiah.

But what about the subtle superstar of this Old Testament book, her mother-in-law, Naomi? By some superficial accounts, Naomi seemed like a cranky old woman who just couldn't get over life's hard knocks.

She even told people to call her "Bitter." I can't say that I blame her. She's comfortable living among like-minded people in Israel until the famine hits. Then her husband takes her and their two sons to a foreign country. The sons eventually marry, then her husband dies, then her sons die. She is alone and penniless.

Not only did she lose the ones she loved, but her livelihood, retirement, and way of life were also gone. All she held dear on earth was gone, and there was very little to look forward to as she looked ahead. In her aged and bereft condition, she decides to head back to the country she left years earlier.

Upon her return, she is defeated and has nowhere else to turn. What a homecoming.

In spite of her bleak inventory, she had hope in the Lord, and it's that nitty-gritty hope that inspired another woman to put her hope in the Lord.

Consider Ruth's famous line: "I won't leave you. Where you go, I'll go, where you stay, I'll stay. Your people will be my people, and your God will be my God." The magnificence of Ruth's stout heart is captivating but look more deeply at the recipient of that devotion.

Put yourself in Ruth's sandals for a moment: Would you devote yourself completely to someone who had nothing to offer and whose presence promised nothing but physical hardship? I think if we were honest, few of us would give up even a nominally comfortable existence to be a companion for someone who named herself "Bitter."

Maybe Ruth had grown very weary of her Moabite environment. Maybe Naomi and Ruth had such intimate conversations about men, marriage, and life that they were kindred spirits. Maybe Naomi understood Ruth's childless misery and had been an encouragement to her when no one else was. Maybe Ruth kept a promise to her husband to take care of Naomi after he had died. Maybe Naomi was the only person who told her about God.

Maybe Ruth knew she needed Naomi more than Naomi needed Ruth.

Whatever the reason, Naomi was very special to Ruth, and vice versa. That kind of a bond doesn't happen overnight but is nurtured through years of kindness, forgiveness, intention, patience, goodness, prayer and being Christ-like. Maybe after loving Naomi so deeply for so long, Ruth could not imagine life without her beloved mentor, mother-in-law and dear friend.

In spite of insurmountable obstacles, Ruth chose to be with her aged mother-in-law because she felt God's love through her.

Naomi breathed **1 Timothy 1:5 – "But the goal of our instruction is love from a pure heart and a good conscience and a sincere faith."** It was this embodiment that attracted Ruth to embrace the God of Naomi and caused her to leave everything behind so she could walk with one who walked with The One.

Wouldn't you like to be the kind of woman like Naomi whose faith through unbearable earthly sufferings is a magnet to Christ? I know I would. I would love to have such magnetic perceptible faith in Christ that another woman would run to Him. I would love to have honest connections, unbridled transparency, and continual meaningful friendship. I would love to be able to say I'm unhappy with the circumstances God has allowed in my life, but I still love Him because He is my everything.

I would love to know someone else is safe enough with me to say, "I'm unhappy with the circumstances God is allowing in my life, but I still love Him because He is my everything," and knows I get her. I would love to be loved and to love like Naomi and Ruth.

Father God, thank you for the friendship of Naomi and Ruth. Thank You that Naomi was brutally honest in her suffering and that You gave her a friend when she needed one. Help me be like Naomi, a woman whose walk with You is so meaningful that someone would give up everything to follow You. Help me be like Ruth, a loyal, encouraging friend. Thank You for my friends and that they love me in spite of my imperfections. Help me to nurture the relationships You've provided, so they are infused with eternal substance. Help me encourage those around me in Christ and help me be thick-skinned, so I can be the kind of friend You want me to be. Thank you for the friendships You are orchestrating for my friends and me in Heaven. Thank You for Your abiding friendship, Lord. I love You.

Mite-y Fine

And He looked up and saw the rich putting their gifts into the treasury. And He saw a certain poor widow putting in two small copper coins. And He said, "Truly I say to you, this poor widow put in more than all of them; for they all out of their surplus put into the offering; but she out of her poverty put in all that she had to live on." ~ Luke 21:1-4

I don't often think of the Lord as an accountant, but He is a great one. He takes account not only of financial offerings but offerings of the heart.

The lavish grace of Jesus is beautifully displayed in the account of the widow's offering. His appreciation for her sacrifice is deeply moving. In the midst of opportunistic offerings, how refreshing it must have been for the Lord to see someone giving sacrificially from the heart and not expecting anything in return. How refreshing it must have been for that devout widow to be defended.

While the puny in spiritual character were incapable of seeing her greatness, the spiritual giant could see she gave with all her heart. And it delighted His heart beyond measure.

In the midst of living in a culture that says bigger is better when was the last time you heard applause for someone

- turning the other cheek

- not returning evil for evil
- obeying a difficult boss
- submitting to the authority of an impossible parent
- going without so someone else can have something
- loving someone who is unlovely
- getting a raise for being a peacemaker
- forgiving someone who hurt you deeply

Consider the seemingly insignificant acts done by people in your church family. Though their small acts seem like nothing compared to a showy venue or a prominent sermon, maybe it was all that persevering saint could offer in light of a spirit drenched in sorrow or a near-empty bank account.

Like the highway warning sign that says "give 'em a break," those who seem like only pew warmers may have a fire burning bright because they are giving generously and forgiving from their heart in ways no one but the Lord sees.

It is an encouragement to know that their master accountant is taking stock of their enormous deposits and that such deposits are mighty fine in His heavenly ledger.

Father God, You are Lord of all and You are intimately aware of how hard it can be to do the right thing when it's just between You and me. Thank You that You are so sincere and appreciative of things done from the heart. Help me to remember that You are my most important audience and may everything I say, think and do glorify Your Name. In Jesus' Name, amen.

Newtonian Physics

A friend loves at all times. ~ *Proverbs 17:17*

"A sincerer or more affectionate friend no man ever had." - William Cowper on describing his beloved pastor, counselor, and friend, John Newton

Don't you just love sermons that pack a wallop? I remember one from over 20 years ago by an earnest Christian gentleman named James Lee. Drawing from the life of David, Dr. Lee declared that "friendship is the celebration of goodness."

Indeed, there are few things sweeter in life than two hearts knit together. I learned about a lesser known dynamic duo through an excellent book by John Piper called The Hidden Smile of God. An evangelical who has earned the right to be heard, Piper insightfully recounts the meaningful friendship between John Newton and William Cowper. Sons of the 18th-century evangelical awakening, their relationship crooned the amazing grace needed for two hearts to celebrate the goodness that God offers lonely souls.

The more familiar of the two, Newton was a shepherd whose aim wasn't just to be respected, but to love and be loved. A pastor's pastor, he received the least of the least with expectancy, believing an interesting message from God was to be revealed in each exchange.

Newton's childlike faith in his heavenly Father expressed complete dependence, awe, belief, and relief. This energetic momentum set in motion a force that couldn't be reckoned with when it came to how he related to people.

Such a powerful force is the stuff that infuses friendship.

Just as relationships require thick skin, they require a healthy dose of seasoning. Just as people go through seasons, so do relationships. A growing friendship is like taking a dose of liquid sunshine - it fills the heart and mind with relief, wholeness, and warmth. On the other hand, a detaching friendship is like taking a bitter pill - it fills the heart and mind with anxiety, loneliness, and coldness.

Being the perfect Friend, Christ provides the wisdom to weather any season of friendship: just love at all times. Sometimes those we love go through difficulties they can't talk about and withdrawal. When that happens, it takes help from on high to continue to be receptive and accepting when they come around.

Sometimes we need people to love us when our tank is empty. Sometimes we need friends to believe in us when we believe lies about ourselves.

Cowper was tragically mentally and emotionally unstable most of his adult life, but Newton loved him. He walked through valleys of depression, social withdrawals and suicide attempts with his friend. Prayerful intercession lead Newton to propose to Cowper that they pen hymns which resulted in the beautiful Olney Hymns. Being the poet laureate of the evangelical awakening, Cowper was the best man for the job, but he needed a friend to receive him, fill his tank and believe in him.

While it may seem that Cowper needed Newton more than Newton needed Cowper, I wonder if it were the other way around. Perhaps Cowper's condition helped Newton be mindful of his own needfulness before the Lord. This helped him be sensitive to **encourage the fainthearted (1 Thes. 5:14).** Furthermore, Newton simply enjoyed the loyalty of a grateful man. Their mutual affection brought new gravity to their personalities and deepened their spiritual dimensions. What a gift!

There was a dark season in my adult life when God moved a

friend to give me a friend. My college Bible study leader, Christie, connected me with a lady in her church, Lin, who had been through a similar dark season and came through it victoriously.

Even though Lin and I lived thousands of miles apart, she called me weekly, wrote me sweet cards, sent me gifts and prayed for me. Several years later and still thousands of miles apart, our hearts are knit together by the Savior we adore as we keep praying for each other, call or email weekly, share our hearts deeply and have our cups overflowed by His goodness.

Jesus Christ mercifully brought me a like-minded friend when I truly need one. The One who mightily works in our hearts powers the kind of relational Newtonian physics that we treasure.

Dear Father, thank you for letting love and friendship happen. Thank You for loving us so we can love each other. Thank You for the friends You have graciously given me who loved me in all kinds of seasons long and brief, painful and joyful. Thank You for weathering the storms of life with me so I can weather storms with people I love. Help me be a better friend like You. In Jesus' Name, amen.

No Orange Sauce

*But now that you have come to know God,
or rather to be known by God, how can you
turn back again to the weak and worthless
elementary principles of the world, whose slaves
you want to be once more?* ~ *Galatians 4:9*

There's a local Chinese restaurant that knows my husband's voice well enough that when he calls in for egg foo young, the owners say, "And no orange sauce." It usually comes with the dish, but Daniel just doesn't care for the sauce, and the owners know this. While anonymity sometimes has advantages, having a restaurant owner get to know you has appetizing value, too.

Letting a restaurant owner know if you like orange sauce is one thing, but being studied and figured out by the owner can be something entirely different. Being in the driver's seat can be empowering in any relationship, but when you feel like the passenger, there's something a bit unnerving – unless the driver is safe and trustworthy.

A Korean preacher said it well in a sermon I heard years ago: "Friendship is the celebration of goodness." It takes goodness to be the kind of person with whom others want to let their guard down. And isn't that what we long for...to be transparent, to feel safe, to be loved...*to be known.*

I appreciate that David was known as a man after God's own heart. He wasn't a man after a busy calendar full of religious activity. He wasn't a man trying to execute perfect plans. He was a man driven to know the heart of God. He successfully knew his Lord intimately, but more importantly, he knew that God knew him. It was God's covenant with David that made all the difference in his life.

And it's God's abiding covenant with you through Christ that makes all the difference in your life today.

As you wait expectantly for the Lord to act in your life, consider how Christ knows you:

- **And even the very hairs of your head are all numbered. Matthew 10:30** (*He knows you intimately*)
- **"I have engraved you on the palms of my hands." Isaiah 49:16** (*He closely watches you*)
- **"For I know the plans I have for you," declares the LORD, "plans to prosper you and not to harm you, plans to give you hope and a future." Jeremiah 29:11** (*He has a good plan*)
- **He will rejoice over you with gladness; he will quiet you by his love; he will exult over you with loud singing. Zephaniah 3:17** (*He knows when you need to be loved on*)

Let these personal truths dwell in you richly as you let your guard down with the Lord. He knows you better than you know yourself, He has your front and your back, and He promises to give you the desires of your heart as you wait on Him.

Father God, You are very great. Your ways are not my ways, and Your thoughts are not like mine. Help me to grasp how wide, long, high and deep Your love is for me. I invite You into those tiny parts of my heart that no one knows about. I long for Your love and companionship because You are good always. Help me to keep my eyes fixed on You, Lord.

In Jesus' Name, amen.

Out of the Blue

Ever have those moments when someone comes to mind out of the blue?

Several years ago I was going about my usual routine at home, when out of nowhere, my former boss popped into my head. I hadn't thought of him for years. I recalled thinking this was odd since we hadn't had contact for years. At the time, I dismissed any thought of him and simply considered it a random fluke. A few years later, I learned that his church had gone through some difficulties. As a result, he had made major changes to his life.

It took me a few days to realize that his major life changes and the "out of the blue" thought I'd had of him occurred simultaneously. When this realization occurred, I understood that instead of dismissing any importance of him coming to mind, I should have prayed for him. He was going through a difficult time, and while I didn't know details of that difficulty, he needed someone to pray for him and his family.

I had been graciously prompted by the Holy Spirit to pray but didn't have the discernment to realize He wanted me to pray for someone. Since that intercessory prompting, I've realized that when God puts someone out of the blue on my heart, it's time to lift that person up before His throne.

An example is another former boss who came to mind. Rather than just one time, this other boss came to mind for several days in a row. While I didn't know particulars, I prayed for God to help him, protect him, draw him to Himself, give him wisdom and help him understand God's love for him. The promptings seemed strong many times throughout consecutive days, then abruptly ended.

There have been times when I've woke in the middle of the night with someone on my heart. Instead of rolling over back to sleep, I lift that person up in prayer and trust that God is the One leading me to pray. While I don't know the outcomes for such prayers, I just pray in faith that the Lord is listening and that my prayer avails much through Christ's righteousness.

I know that God has put me on the hearts of others in the wee hours of the morning. One such lady used to pray for me at 4:00 am! I still feel so much love when I think of that.

I've moved 17 times in my lifetime and have gone through several address books. I've lost touch with more friends and coworkers than I care to share.

Thankfully, God keeps my spiritual address book current.

Every so often, my Heavenly Operator dials up my memory Rolodex, opens my heart to consider a need in someone else and invites me to pray for an old friend. This exchange is a gift.

I've learned to appreciate that folks don't come to mind just out of the blue. They are placed on my heart for a season of prayer, and that is one call I don't want to miss.

Pauline

"In everything I showed you that by working hard in this matter you must help the weak and remember the words of the Lord Jesus, that He Himself said, 'It is more blessed to give than to receive.'" Paul to the Ephesian Church Elders in Acts 20:35

My Grandma Pauline made an impression on many people during her lifetime. She was industrious and talented. Her busy hands were constantly creating through sewing or crocheting or cooking. She loved making clothes or blankets for her grandchildren, and she taught me how to sew. Her friendships provided much-needed companionship and helped to softened her parched heart. She often took me to lunch when I was a college student.

And her unique way of eating grapefruit has sliced its way to a third generation as my son only eats grapefruit as I taught him the way my grandma taught me.

Giving back was important to my grandma, and it was vitally important to the apostle Paul. Giving saturated his lifestyle, but it didn't happen overnight. Refinement to our Christian character does not occur in an instant. There are seasons of valleys and mountaintops that soften our rough edges to make us more like our Savior as we yield to His will.

The Lord's mission for Saul was clear from the beginning: **to**

suffer for Christ's name's sake (Acts 9:16). While you and I won't have the tough job of suffering as an early church father, there are lessons from Paul's life that mirror ours and provide insight into the maturity of every believer, including church leaders.

Without a doubt, the reaching out of fellow believers like Ananias and Barnabas enveloped Paul and provided the loving environment needed for thriving. In spite of internal and external opposition, these men came alongside Paul, and their godly influence planted a fragrant aroma in his heart and the hearts of other believers as they opened their lives to their former persecutor.

Like Elijah did with Elisha, Paul poured himself out like a drink offering into the lives of God's people. He **sought the Lord for direction (Galatians 1:16)** and **trusted in His goodness even when it was uncomfortable (2 Corinthians 12:7).** Paul's seeking and trusting in the Lord enabled men like Timothy and Titus to entrust their lives to him. **Proverbs 14:26 says "In the fear of the Lord there is strong confidence. And his children will have refuge."** Paul's spiritual children felt safe and secure, and they drew closer to the Lord as a result.

It is so cool to see the growth of Paul from one of his earliest books, Galatians, to his final book, Romans. In his final remarks to the Galatians, there isn't any recognition or thanks or greeting offered to or from anyone in particular. By contrast, Romans is oozing with recognition and appreciation for over 15 people for their service and fellowship! Wow.

Perhaps Paul knew his time was coming to an end, and that motivated him to speak from his heart. Or perhaps Paul was a man just like us who learned that ministry wasn't just about him but was about really **knowing his flock (2 Timothy 1:4).**

Perhaps Paul learned that ministry was more fulfilling being with the people who looked up to him for love and affirmation, rather than shutting himself off in a room to just write sermons (**Acts 28:30**).

Perhaps Paul learned that being a minister isn't about having people offer applause, but about applauding them so others can follow their example (**Philippians 2:25-29**). He seemed like a lonely man at times and was hungry for human company (**Acts 20:11**).

Paul was the first to admit his flaws. It's strangely comforting to see his imperfect life played out in scripture. It helps to understand that Paul was a work in progress like me, like every other believer and like those whom I love who have yet to call on the Lord to be saved.

Can you relate to the Pauline struggle for wholeness in **Romans 7:24: "Wretched man that I am! Who will set me free from the boy of this death? Thanks be to God through Jesus Christ our Lord!"** It's my mantra.

Father God, You are full of grace and mercy. You are a good, good Father whose love endures forever. Thank You for helping Paul to finish the race You called him to run. Even when it was hard for him, he stayed on track. Help me be like Paul. Help me make myself available to others in love, in cheerfulness and holy sacrifice. Help me to rely on Your strength like Paul did so that You get all the praise and glory as only You deserve. In Jesus' Name, amen.

Red Dog

"Take my yoke upon you and learn from me, for I am gentle and humble in heart, and you will find rest for your souls." ~ Matthew 11:29

I watched a feel-good movie not too long ago called "Red Dog." It's based on the true story about a dog who is embraced by a small town called Dampier in Western Australia. There's not much going on in Dampier during the 1970s except a lot of industry and dust, so it's no wonder a charming stray dog wanders into their hearts. The dog is named Red Dog. While Red Dog's amicable presence serves as a buffer between the harsh reality of tough work and loneliness for many, we learn that something is missing in Red Dog's life: a master.

In a pivotal scene, Red Dog entertains a large group. After he gorges an entire can of dog food in 9.2 seconds, they bring out a live chicken for Red Dog to devour. As the frenzied crowd goes wild with anticipation, the local bus driver, John, walks into the bar and senses that Red Dog does not want to comply. The dog longingly looks to John to rescue him. John realizes he needs to help Red Dog. After some tense negotiation, he persuades the crowd to stop hounding the poor dog. John then leaves the bar with his new best four-footed friend.

A few years later, John is killed in a motorcycle accident, but Red Dog is relentless in trying to find him. The dog reportedly went all over Western Australia looking for John. Eventually, Red Dog makes his way back to Dampier, and the town erects a statue in honor of the loyal pooch since he embodied such a generous spirit.

While there weren't any obvious religious overtones in the story, I couldn't help but think the relationship between John and Red Dog is a microcosm of our relationship to God.

We do life with a sense of something missing until that Someone becomes everything to us.

For Red Dog, because he didn't have one master, he was, in a sense, slave to all.

He provided some mutually satisfying reprieve for bored people, but he also was live bait when idleness crept in during non-working hours for bored people.

Red Dog proved he could keep everyone happy for a little while through speedily consuming a can of dog food. He seemed to understand the high stakes when a live chicken was brought in: he would have to tap into something dangerous inside himself to satisfy the crowd he was slave to. They wanted that insatiable brutality to be fed.

When John mercifully stepped in to save Red Dog from becoming a monster, the dog was eternally grateful and would never be the same again. I think the crowd was also grateful for John's intervention because it curbed their own wanton rebellion.

Isn't it like that with Christ? He sees the dangerous consequence of sin around us and in us. Thankfully, He doesn't stand by without trying to intervene:

- **He has a heart that longs to gather us like a hen gathers her chicks under her wings (Matthew 23:37)**
- **He stands at the door and knocks to come into our hearts (Revelation 3:20)**
- **I slept but my heart was awake. Listen! It is the voice of my beloved who knocks (Song of Songs 5:2)**

Jesus is our merciful rescuer through delivering us from ourselves. He knows the latent brutality inside each of us. Without taking His gentle yoke and being in agreement with Him that we desperately need His help, we are doomed to feed our sinful nature because it is a restless beast. Red Dog loved John not only for rescuing him that night, but for rescuing him from becoming a hated monster.

Titus 3:3 says, "At one time we too were foolish, disobedient, deceived and enslaved by all kinds of passions and pleasures. We lived in malice and envy, *being hated and hating one another.*"

Just as John became Red Dog's everything, Jesus becomes our everything as we habitually take His loving yoke upon ourselves.

Lord God, You are Savior of the world. You are humble and gentle of heart, and I take Your yoke upon me. When I have chosen to take Your yoke off, please forgive me and remind me that Yours is light. Thank You for rescuing me from myself. I am grateful for Your patience with me and for being my master. I am Your servant, and I love You with all that I am. In Jesus' Name, amen.

Reluctant Wrestler

***And a man wrestled with Jacob until the
breaking of the day. ~ Genesis 32:24***

"Athlete by nature. Wrestler by choice" This phrase caught my eye on
a t-shirt at a wrestling meet. I watched my first live match when my
son started wrestling in middle school. It was pretty fun until I saw
bodies twist and turn in ways that I had only seen in a pretzel. Boys
looked upon my boy like he was prey. And my boy was transformed
into a predator.

The hunt was on as they advanced toward one another. Arms
locked, bodies pinned and there was no way out until someone
yielded. It seemed painful in more ways than one, but one thing
the wrestlers had in common was that they participated by choice.

We're all wrestlers by choice whether it's on the mat or in our
minds. We wrestle with decisions. We wrestle in relationships. We
wrestle at our jobs. We wrestle with doing the good thing or doing
the best thing. And we wrestle with God.

Take the Bible's favorite man of the mat, Jacob. His t-shirt
might've read something like "Shark by nature. Wrestler by choice."
He was the master of shrewdness – from cooking up a stealthy
menu to steal his brother's birthright to taking his father-in-law out
to pasture by breeding a stronger herd. It wasn't enough that Jacob
outsmarted the competition, but he seemed to look for opportunities
to show others who was the boss. Even with a supernatural being.

While Jacob's posturing in this instance may seem presumptuous, what's more surprising is that Jacob's invitation to engage the divine was even accepted. Serious students of Scripture have debated who wrestled with Jacob that night. Was it the Lord, an angel or a man? Before this encounter under the stars, Jacob had been interacting with the Lord during his journey home, so it seems that this wrestling match was made in Heaven. I'm not a biblical scholar, but if God wanted us to know for sure who wrestled with Jacob, I think He would have made it clear.

Since the text isn't clear on this point, I think what God wanted to emphasize is that when we want to wrestle with His plan, He accepts. It is amazing to me that the Holy One would be willing, let alone even listen, to such a request.

What is also amazing is His grace. Because of it, we can go "mano a mano" with the God of all creation. It would seem that by accepting a wrestler's challenge, God needs to prove something. But nothing could be further from the truth. God has nothing to prove to us, but in wrestling with us, He allows us to engage with Him in a very raw way. We can be brutally honest with Him (what we say wouldn't surprise Him anyway). He knows we need a safe place where we can pour out our hearts to express our longings, struggles, losses and agony.

He prefers our authenticity and transparency anyway, so maybe getting us to wrestle with Him is His way of actually enjoying fellowship in a culture of disingenuous religious activity (**Isaiah 1:10-20**)!

Whether we wrestle one night with the Lord and are forever changed like Jacob was, or whether we wrestle over the course of years to come to a deeper relationship, wrestling with God results in losing something because He will always win. But in so losing, we win. Jesus said, **"For whoever wants to save their life will lose it, but whoever loses their life for me will find it." (Matthew 16:25)**

I guess if I were to design my own t-shirt, it'd be something like " Reluctant wrestler by choice."

By this I mean that I'm hesitant to engage in something I would rather avoid, even wrestling with God. I've gone "mano a mano" with the Lord over more disappointments than I care to rehearse. But through these times, I've learned that, ultimately, every struggle is with God because, in His glorious mysterious sovereignty, He allows trials.

There are easier, more predictable seasons to be sure, and I am very thankful for those. But when those tough seasons come, I have joyfully learned to embrace the One who allows both, appreciating what Peter said, **"Lord, to whom shall we go? You have the words of eternal life." (John 6:68)**

Yieldedness to the Victor even in apparent loss results in an incomparable sweetness that bears much good fruit in time.

Father God, Your love is better than life itself. You are far more wiser and intelligent than I can grasp, and I am thankful You know all things. Thank You for letting me wrestle with You when I struggle, and thank You for the joy that comes in yielding to You. Increase my faith so I will more wholeheartedly long for Your kingdom to come and for Your will to be done on earth as it is in Heaven. In Jesus' Name, amen.

Seasoning

I know what it is to be in need, and I know what it is to have plenty. I have learned the secret of being content in any and every situation, whether well-fed or hungry, whether living in plenty or in want. ~ Phillippians 4:12

I live in a climate that hosts four seasons, but I only welcome three of them. Even though I've grown pretty content as a 10 year Wisconsin transplant, I loathe winter every year. This annual dread hits me when I shovel my driveway after the first snowfall. And after the second snowfall, then the third, seventh, tenth and so on. It hits me when my happy lead foot must sadly slow down in icy driving conditions. It hits my husband when I logically explain my annual reasons for retiring where the seasons never change and where we could enjoy warm, sunny skies all year long.

It's like that in the seasons of life, too. I posture myself before the Almighty and give valid reasons why I shouldn't have to endure harsh climates of loneliness, rejection, transition, loss, and silence.

It doesn't seem fair to lose a comfortable job and paycheck. It doesn't seem fair to have to maintain a lifelong disease. It doesn't seem fair to start over when the getting was just getting good. It doesn't seem fair when you're left out in the cold, and everyone else seems to have it all warm and cozy.

Like the intense climate of a harsh desert valley, so it feels in the unwelcomed seasons of life. There is a complicatedness of trusting in the One who allows the difficulty while pleading your case for the desert living to end as painlessly and as quickly as possible.

My cycle of seasons goes something like this: I walk, run, fall, get up, cry, find someone safe to talk to, shout at God, scream why me, wipe my tears, cry some more, laugh sometimes, run again, trip and get up the hundredth time, talk more, shout more, find joy in who God is, acknowledge the goodness of God to Him and to others through all that stuff, find rest as I give Him my burdens...and when I can see the "exit this way" sign on the horizon, I take a big breath and sigh of relief as I soak in His sweet faithfulness poured out.

Ultimately, there is a relief as I understand what it means to share in His sufferings. Afterward, as I envelope myself under His wings, I dream again and enjoy the luxury of risk to make myself vulnerable again.

Take Me Out to the Ball Game

I bought my first professional baseball tickets when I was 45. It was because of my Dad. He wanted to see the Brewers play at Miller Park in Milwaukee when he came to visit my family and me in southern Wisconsin. How could I say no? I thought I got a good deal on tickets sitting near third base. It didn't seem like such a good deal when the sun was shining in our eyes during the ninth inning and when I realized I left the sunscreen at home. We had fun anyway, and the trip made my Dad happy.

Not to be confused with a box of chocolates, but life is like a baseball game. Just when you think you're about to hit a home run, you strike out. Or you hit a foul ball. But no matter how many strikeouts, fly outs, tag outs and force outs you may have, thankfully **nothing can ever separate us from the love of God (Romans 8:38)!**

One seemingly minor figure in the Old Testament was a major player in God's divine plan. She gracefully hung in there through thick and thin. Her name was Hannah. And she was a winner who hit a lot of home runs because of her faith in God. She still suffered many blows but her **God gave her all she needed for life and godliness (2 Peter 1:3).**

When I took a look at the life of the prophet Samuel, I couldn't help but look at the life of his mother, Hannah. I admit I don't understand polygamy in the Old Testament, but Hannah was part of a polygamous union. Her husband, Elkanah, had two wives, the other named Peninnah.

It appears that Peninnah was not like her name (meaning "pearl," something precious). Peninnah had many children, but Hannah had none. Peninnah reminded Hannah often of her barren condition. Peninnah seemed to relish in her rival's grief. We don't know much more about Peninnah but her example reminds me that sometimes even God's people sinfully enjoy being cruel.

First Samuel 1:7 says that Elkanah took his family to offer temple sacrifices year after year. Each time, Peninnah provoked Hannah to the point of tears and losing her appetite. What is interesting is that Hannah never did anything mean in return to Peninnah. She was **entrusting herself to her faithful Creator (1 Peter 4:19)**. What is also interesting is that God didn't rebuke Hannah for crying her eyes out in her unbearable suffering and bitter sorrow.

Instead of turning away from God in rage, it's important to realize that Hannah turned toward God and poured out her heart before Him. They say you become like what you worship, and Hannah's example of being truly gracious to an ungracious woman is evidence of that.

Hannah was **not put to shame for trusting in the Lord (Psalm 25:3)**. Even the priest, Eli, didn't think much of this poor lovely lady. As she was weeping and praying in the temple for her own treasured child to love, Eli accused her of being a drunk! Even in the frustration of feeling alone and empty, Hannah maintains her composure, explains her prayers and defends her integrity. She was not ashamed to testify that her hope was in the Lord. Eli must have seen her godly character and regretted his remarks by blessing her with the promise of a son.

Verse 1:20 says that "in due time" Hannah conceived. Could it be that, like Jacob when he finally married Rachel, all those years of waiting seemed like just a few days to Hannah?

While Samuel was certainly a great reward for Hannah, **her song of praise affirms her greatest reward, the Lord (2:1-10).** Her years of waiting on Him intensified her longing and made its actualization sweeter.

The Lord refined Hannah as she waited on Him and obeyed Him, even when she was provoked - in church, no less!

The Lord had a plan to bring Samuel on the scene when He did: Israel needed strong leadership during its infancy kingdom stage. Not only did Samuel deliver respectable and faithful leadership, he was so loved throughout his life as its prophet, that **all of Israel mourned him when he died (1 Samuel 25:1).**

I doubt Samuel would have been as effective without the influence of a godly, praying mother who took seriously the small things like turning the other cheek to be a peacemaker. His mom also took seriously a huge promise she made to the Lord by giving her one and only son to serve Him all his days.

Whether you're a mother or not, male or female, young or old, the life of Hannah is one to be greatly admired.

While it seemed like her barren existence kept her in the dugout, God had her there for His purposes. Hannah's amazing faith was deeply appreciated by the God **who gave back to her what the locust had eaten (Joel 2:25) and restored her fortunes before her eyes (Zephaniah 3:20). First Samuel 7:17 says that Samuel returned to his home at Ramah where he built an altar.** Put another way, Samuel returned to his Mama at Ramah! I'd say they both hit a home run straight out of the ballpark.

Father God, thank You for Hannah. Thank You for Hannah's faith and how she trusted in Your unfailing goodness. Thank You for not only being her defender, strength, provider, and deliverer but mine also. I know that You love me, and I am so grateful to be Yours. Help me in my faith when I feel like I'm in the dugout of life and not able to play ball the way I want to. Your promises are worth clinging to anywhere in any season of life. In Jesus' Name, Amen.

The Philemon Challenge

I was 14 when I decided to get my first tattoo. My mom was clueless about our scheme when she dropped my friend, Halle, and me off at the Springfield Mall one quiet fall afternoon. We told her we would do some shopping and looked forward to being picked up several hours later.

As my parents' 1979 vanilla cream colored two-door Buick Regal trustingly drove away, Halle and I coasted towards the Metro bus stop and waited anxiously for our colorful date with destiny at a tattoo parlor in bustling Georgetown. Once we boarded the bus to transport us into DC, we felt a rush of naughty, magical, youthful adrenaline. Not only were we in stealth mode, but we were on the verge of taking a rite of passage into adulthood. We'd kept this adventure to ourselves, and our plucky spirits were soaring. Our exploit unfolding, we felt on top of the world and were as thick as thieves!

Not exactly the most wholesome memory to unleash, but it conjures up a time of connecting with my first best friend from high school and feeling kind of special. Our quest to simultaneously alter our skin that day left a mark that is still etched as a one and only kind of thrill to a one and only friend during a one and only season.

Being someone's one and only removes any reminder of wanting to be someone else. Being someone's one and only stops you from backing life up. Being someone's one and only makes you feel like someone.

Long ago, a somebody named Paul wrote a little letter to another somebody named Philemon telling him to take a nobody named Onesimus and treat him like he was somebody.

Philemon commanded respect wherever he went. Paul's apostolic moxie tapped Philemon's prominence. This influence was to be poured out on someone who needed to be reminded that he was ***His*** one and only. Confident of his friend's response, the result glorified God. Philemon restored his wayward servant, Onesimus. Godly transformation took root in a needy man who desperately needed assurance, reconciliation, and companionship.

Onesimus had nothing of great importance to offer in return. He had no earthly status, wealth or prominence. He was a slave, a nobody in the eyes of the world. But he meant the world to His Creator. And his Creator called upon someone to help Onesimus clearly understand that he was indeed someone precious, respected and dearly loved.

Sounds like the task the Lord Jesus took on when He accepted His Father's important call to redeem lost, wayward, empty souls like yours and mine. We were slaves to sin when He graciously forgave us. His rescuing arms affirm us as His beloved.

Fortunately, my adventure with Halle wasn't an isolated incident of feeling like someone's one and only. Thankfully, since becoming a Christian, God brought His saints my way who accepted the "Philemon Challenge" to help me feel like a somebody, especially when I wasn't somebody's one and only anymore.

They listened attentively, they hugged without words, they made themselves available when it wasn't convenient, they sent me sweet notes in the mail, they prayed with and for me, and their simple acts of sacrificial love made me feel like I was 10 feet tall! In short, I felt His love through them. That helped me draw nearer to the One whose love is inexhaustible, complete, perfect, satisfying and so worth it.

Everybody knows of a nobody who is aching to be somebody... who is in your circle or your church or your family who needs extra love? What if you spent precious time investing in that individual and made her your one and only even for a one and only season...give it time and invest your patience and gentleness and love.

Afraid to let someone needy become attached? Remember that someone, somewhere at some time did it for you, or will in your unknown time of need.

Afraid of getting burned by someone who seems to have a scorching need? Remember **Isaiah 43:2 - He is with you in the fire.**

Be God with skin on anyway. Take the "Philemon Challenge" and make someone your one and only.

Speaking of skin, when Halle and I finally arrived to get our tattoos, we suddenly thought, "What will our tattoos look like when we're 80?" Sadly, the Georgetown tattoo parlor owner didn't count on two reckless 14-year-old girls apply reason after their extensive trek to the nation's capitol. Surprisingly, we did. I'm so glad we followed our thoughtful advice that day.

Funny how an inkling of unselfish behavior can transform a heart into something worth writing home about.

The Sweetest Thing

I had the privilege of serving at Lifest in Oshkosh, Wisconsin. Lifest is a four-day July gathering of Christian bands and entertainers. It's promoted as "A Party with a Purpose." You should check it out. Not having been to Lifest before, I didn't know what to expect.

I knew we'd give away lots of books at our table, but I didn't know we'd have so many wonderful conversations with people who love Jesus. I knew we'd hear cool music, but I didn't know how meaningful the musicians' messages would be during their concerts. I knew there'd be entertainment, but I didn't know that each venue would be intentionally sharing the gospel.

I didn't know how thirsty my soul was till it was drenched in grace, and oh how sweetly He showered me in it.

Crowded venues really aren't my thing, but when an opportunity comes along to share what the Lord is doing, I want to go. There were thousands of people at Lifest, and I was glad my son was there with me. Since another volunteer was working with us, we were able to enjoy some of what the weekend had to offer in between passing out free books.

I heard Skillet for the first time and never knew something in me would actually like Christian hard rock, but I did. I cried when Casting Crowns sang my favorite song, "Who Am I". I belted out and danced to "Jesus Freak" with the Newsboys. I heard wonderful testimonies of what God is doing in people's lives and learned that hundreds of people put their faith in Jesus at Lifest.

It was such an encouraging and uplifting time, but I'd have to say the sweetest thing was feeling God's love through and with my son.

Like I said, crowded venues aren't my cup of tea. After 48 hours of talking with hundreds of people and being away from home, I was feeling tired during the second evening. If you're like me, being tired when it's late can be tense, especially for my family. I snapped at my son when he said it was time for us to leave the Casting Crowns concert, then I gave into my fleshly desire, lost control of my tongue and regretfully said some unkind words.

Thankfully, we resolved things before going to bed, but I still felt lousy about it in the morning. As I apologized again to my son, I started to cry, and he graciously said, "It's ok, Mom. I forgive you because I love you so much. You don't need to feel bad." My heart melted, my spirit soared, and I felt such relief. I knew I had been forgiven, and it. felt. absolutely. AWESOME!

As I look back at the final concert, I was able to worship the Lord with abandon because I was mercifully given a taste of how good He is to a wretched sinner like me. And next to me was the apple of my eye singing his heart out to "We Believe":

"We believe in God the Father
We believe in Jesus Christ
We believe in the Holy Spirit
And He's given us new life
We believe in the crucifixion
We believe that He conquered death
We believe in the resurrection
And that He's coming back again"

It just doesn't get any sweeter than that. Thank You, Lord! Amen!

Total Forgiveness

Many years ago, someone recommended that I read R.T. Kendall's book, <u>Total Forgiveness</u>. I would notice it in the CBD catalog and had it on my Amazon wish list for a long time. Thirteen years later, I finally got my own copy and am so very thankful for the wisdom God gave Reverend Kendall in producing a helpful, purposeful, insightful and liberating book.

As I agreed with much of what Kendall shared, I wondered why I waited so long to read it. I didn't beat myself up over this, but I sense that I wasn't ready back then for much of what he shared. I may have thrown the book away or simply felt I couldn't do what he encouraged the reader to do - totally forgive.

I think what change I appreciate the most in the past 13 years is how God has graciously revealed Himself to me and is increasing my understanding of how really big and awesome He is!

I'm confident Rev. Kendall's purpose was not to make me feel criminal, but there were times I honestly felt like one when I read his book. Instead of looking for fault in those who have wronged me, I was graciously reminded through his book that my response to being sinned against was no less offensive to a forgiving God who is the only one fit to judge and avenge. By His wounds I am healed!

God's greatest longing is to reconcile the world to Himself. Since He has reconciled me to Him through Christ's blood, withholding forgiveness is not an option. As I was challenged to let go of every bitter grudge, I am embarrassed to admit that I tried to talk myself out of it.

Who would take care of the enormous hurts I've endured if I wasn't still mad? What would I do with all that mental and emotional energy if it couldn't hold onto my anger?

Thankfully, God said He would and that I'd actually feel much better if I let Him direct all my mental and emotional energy for greater purposes than harboring hatred in my crowded heart.

He also reassured me that He would provide a way out when I started to rehearse the hurts and feel indignant when my enemy prospered. He would also remind me that He has kindly forgiven me of all the terrible things I've ever done and that His payment was absolutely perfect in paying the price for all my sin. His hatred for all the sin done to me is real, too, and He paid the price for that, too.

If I could agree with how good it is to not steal or lie, shouldn't I agree with God that unforgiveness is just as wrong and necessary to give up? It made perfect sense. But before its totality would become a habit to motivate me to walk in forgiveness to those knee-jerk offended reactions, it would take some practice and a lot of help.

Always the Great Physician and knowing the fever of unforgiveness could consume me again, Dr. Jesus provided a prescription: **Psalm 51**. I've read this psalm dozens of times, but I had a refreshingly new perspective on it as I read Total Forgiveness.

God had clearly put several people on my heart I needed to not only totally forgive for past and potentially future offenses, but I also needed to ask for Him to bless them. So, the way He showed me to be committed to forgiving and asking for His blessing over them was to insert their names in Psalm 51. It was amazing.

As I prayed for the person by name, I felt lighter and even felt compassion for my offender. I felt like s/he mattered deeply to God and that his/her greatest need, like mine, is to be reconciled to Christ. In short, praying this way for my offenders made me feel at home with Jesus because He seemed to feel at home with me.

I know I will need to take my medicine again and again when

I'm offended or when satan encourages me to get mad over past offenses so this "prescription" is just as much for me as it is for you.

It is my prayer that you and Jesus feel at home with each other as you live in total forgiveness and rely on Him to help you.

Insert your person's name where there Is an _____. Or when you've blown it, insert your name instead. You matter to God, and He wants you to forgive yourself just as much! Don't let satan rob us of joy God has for us through forgiving and being forgiven.

Psalm 51 – Prescription to Totally Forgive

Be gracious to _____, O God, according to Thy lovingkindness;
According to the greatness of Thy compassion blot out _____'s transgressions.
Wash _____ thoroughly from his/her iniquity, and cleanse _____ from his/her sin.
For _____ knows her/his transgressions, and her/his sin is ever before her/him. Against Thee, and Thee only, has _____ sinned, and done what is evil in Thy sight,
So that Thou art justified when Thou dost speak, and blameless when Thou dost judge.
Behold, _____ was brought forth in iniquity, and in sin his/her mother conceived _____. Behold, Thou dost desire truth in the innermost being,
And in the hidden part Thou wilt make _____ know wisdom.
Purify _____ with hyssop, and _____ shall be clean;
Wash _____, and _____ shall be whiter than snow.
Make _____ to hear joy and gladness,
Let the bones which Thou hast broken rejoice.
Hide Thy face from _____'s sins,
And blot out all _____'s iniquities.
Create in _____ a clean heart, O God,
And renew a steadfast spirit within _____.

Do not cast _____ away from Thy presence,

And do not take Thy Holy Spirit from _____.

Restore to _____ the joy of Thy salvation,

And sustain _____ with a willing spirit.

Then _____ will teach transgressors Thy ways,

And sinners will be converted to Thee.

Deliver _____ from bloodguiltiness, O God, Thou God of
_____'s salvation;

Then _____'s tongue will joyfully sing of Thy righteousness.

O Lord, open _____'s lips,

That _____'s mouth may declare Thy praise,

For Thou dost not delight in sacrifice, otherwise _____
would give it.

Thou art not pleased with burnt offering.

The sacrifices of God are a broken spirit;

A broken and a contrite heart, O God, Thou wilt not despise.

By Thy favor do good to Zion;

Build the walls of Jerusalem,

Then Thou wilt delight in righteous sacrifices,

In burnt offering and whole burnt offering;

Then young bulls will be offered on Thine altar.

What I Need...

No one listens to me...I need a voice louder than mine
**After it his voice roars; he thunders with his
majestic voice, and he does not restrain the
lightning when his voice is heard. Job 37:4**

I don't love like I should...I need a heart bigger than mine
**The steadfast love of the LORD never ceases;
his mercies never come to an end.
Lamentations 3:22**

I'm weak...I need muscles stronger than mine
In him all things hold together. Colossians 1:17

I'm not a good listener...I need ears more attentive than mine
**For the LORD hears the needy and does not despise
his own people who are prisoners. Psalm 69:33**

Sloth is my middle name...I need hands busier than mine
**The LORD is the everlasting God, the Creator of the
ends of the earth. He will not grow tired or weary, and
his understanding no one can fathom. Isaiah 40:28**

I'm slow...I need a mind more engaged than mine

*He will be the sure foundation for your times, a rich
store of salvation and wisdom and knowledge; the fear
of the LORD is the key to this treasure. Isaiah 33:6*

Mine, mine, mine, mine…I need a more generous spirit than mine
*"At that time I will gather you; at that time I will bring
you home. I will give you honor and praise among all the
peoples of the earth when I restore your fortunes before
your very eyes," says the LORD. Zephaniah 3:20*

I don't see others' needs…I need eyes that see more than mine
*For the eyes of the LORD run to and fro throughout
the whole earth, to give strong support to those whose
heart is blameless toward him. 2 Chronicles 16:9*

All I see is this big obstacle…I need Someone
with a greater vision than mine
*And I tell you that you are Peter, and on this
rock I will build my church, and the gates of
Hades will not overcome it. Matthew 16:18*

I am so very tired…I need genuine, lasting rest
*Take my yoke upon you and learn from me, for
I am gentle and humble in heart, and you will
find rest for your souls. Matthew 11:29*

I'm bummed…I need a good laugh
*A cheerful heart is good medicine, but a crushed
spirit dries up the bones. Proverbs 17:22*
She hasn't replied in a long time…I need a faithful Friend
*There is no greater love than to lay down
one's life for one's friends. John 15:13*

I need You, Lord! Help me be more like You, Jesus!

? !

Rejoice always. ~ 1 Thessalonians 5:16
Jesus wept. ~ John 11:35
Be thankful. ~ 1 Thessalonians 5:18
Pray for us. ~ Hebrews 13:18

A few summers ago, I read Victor Hugo's <u>Les Miserables</u> to my son. Together, we despised Javier's relentless unmerciful pursuit of Jean Valjean. We cheered Jean Valjean's victorious merciful treatment of those he touched. We couldn't believe the despicable behavior of the Thenardiers. We survived the never-ending 18-page description of the Battle of Waterloo, then paused with welcomed relief and surprise when Hugo encapsulated it all by quoting General Cambronne.

For such a verbose author, it's surprising that Hugo and his agent exchanged the shortest telegram in perhaps all of history: " *? !*." Hugo had sent the first part (?) by asking how his manuscript had been received, while his agent sent the second part (!) indicating that Les Mis was on its way to becoming a commercial success.

Sometimes the most potent messages come in little packages.

It doesn't take a Victor Hugo to talk to God. And sometimes God is succinct in the way He talks to us. Earnestly just crying out "help me" or "love on me" or "give me wisdom, Lord" must be like music to God's ears because it's from the heart and brings you to complete dependence on Him, which is just where He wants us to be.

A friend once asked me what I want to ask Him when I get Home. I said that I just want to sit on His lap and be held. That simple message from my Heavenly Father will be more powerful than any verbal explanation.

One of my life verses sums up this homecoming longing: **"The Lord, your God, is with you, the Mighty Warrior who saves. He will take great delight in you; in his love he will no longer rebuke you, but will rejoice over you with singing." Zephaniah 3:17**

Help me, Father. I need and love You.

Epilogue

Never in a million years would I dream of having anything in common with a 28-year-old tattooed singer of a Christian metalcore band, but I do! Mike Hranka of the Dayton, Ohio-based band, The Devil Wears Prada, also took five years to write his book, <u>Three Dots and the Guilt Machine</u>. Five years may seem like a lifetime in the publishing world, but I'm grateful for the patience of the folks at Westbow Publishing.

Writing this devotional memoir has been important and meaningful to me. Infused in its pages are many years worth of gains, insights, musings, prayers, meditations, studies, and wrestling that have made me stronger. I wish I could say that in the last five years, all my issues and concerns of life are fully resolved, but I can't. I wish I could offer some sense that spiritual maturity equates perfection, but I can't. I wish I could tell you that all my friendships have become stronger and closer since I started this writing journey, but I can't. I wish I could tell you that everything has been perfectly rosy in my household, but I can't do that either. We've had career and personal changes welcomed and unwelcomed. I wish I could say that life gets easier as you mature in Christ, but to be honest, sometimes it seems harder.

Sometimes life is whizzing along so fast and happy like I'm riding a roller coaster at Six Flags, then there are times when life seems so excruciatingly slow that I wonder if there is any progress happening at all. I heard in a sermon that "Sometimes you go with the pattern even when it feels like the Lord isn't leading." So I go with His pattern, not just with the flow!

What I can tell you is that welcoming Jesus into every eventuality of my life has become normal and common. I've appreciated that no matter how small or trivial a matter is, I can talk to Him about it. "Lord, where are my car keys? I can't find them." to "Lord, how are we going to pay this bill?" to "Lord, I'd really like to take that trip to Cali, but it seems so extravagant." to "Lord, I don't want to love that person. The hurt is too raw."

What I can tell you is that I can't imagine my life without Jesus Christ. I can't imagine an hour without talking to Him. What I can tell you is that in all my introvertedness, quirks, and selective conversation, I have the most welcoming audience with the God of the universe. I talk to Him about everything. He has never ever made me feel unwelcome or unwanted. He has made me feel bad about hurtful things I've done to Him and others, and rightly so. I'm glad I feel bad when I'm naughty, selfish, indifferent and ill-tempered. I'm glad I know I can run to the One whose love is true, honest, uplifting, sincere, amazingly available and absolutely mine.

I'm glad God has taught me that all the special things I've accepted from Him aren't just for me, but are for you, too. His offer is for those who hate me, too. And if His offer isn't for them, then it can't be for me either. *This* is where maturity in Christ gets harder, but even in this, He is faithful to show me 'tis so sweet to trust in Jesus and to make my heart at home with His.

Let your heart be His home, too.

If anything in this book has encouraged you, I would be so touched to hear from you. Please send me a note at brookbesor@gmail.com. Thanks.

Shout Outs

I have been touched by so many awesome people! With special thanks...

Mom – Thanks for saying, "You should be a writer!" And for being there for me when I needed it. I love you!

Dad, Marie, Kasey, Mike, Tom and Whitney – Thanks for being there for me when I needed it. I love you all!

My Faith Community Church family – there's so many of you who have touched me: Pastor Rusty Lyon, John Ackatz, Larry & Lenore Johnson, Sheri Humphrey, Jenny & Erich Utrie, Ed & Eve Solano, Dave & Debbie Johnson, Gary & Cathy Niesen, Tim & Susan Brockmann, Jackie Lyon, Karl & Donna Senger, Eric & Lisa Felth, Rod & Bridget Nesseth, Donna Klevgaard, Becky Bates, Jerry & Shirley Brown, Chad & Erica Sanders, Sherry Myers, Karen Fries, Eric & Jodi Wipperfurth, Dom & Karen Bava, Jim & Nedra Lemke, Diane Saxe, Marsha Wilson, Bethany Wilson, Mary Davis, Dave & Annette Foster, Kim Hollman, Mark & Teri Macejkovic, JoAnn Wilson, Greg & Jeanne Pibal, Don & Jan Christianson, Connie Congdon, and Sandi Partin. Wow – are we blessed or what?! Thank you for sharing your faith and lives with me, and for letting me share mine with you. Praying with you and trusting our Heavenly Father together makes all the difference.

The kind folks at Living Waters Bible Camp in Westby WI who refresh Daniel and me for wonderful weekend get-a-ways: Theo &

Ruth Habel, Dennis & Mary Ann Siler, Chris & Annie Sutton, Andrew Jackson, Tim & Joy Hadley.

Musicians who have inspired and encouraged me: U2 (especially at the Pittsburgh PA Joshua Tree concert with my son), Sara Groves, August Burns Red, Thrice, The Devil Wears Prada, Darkness Divided, Skillet, Jars of Clay, Anne Barbor, David Crowder.

Authors who have touched me: Charles Stanley, Billy Graham, Anne Graham Lotz, Ruth Graham, Stormie Omartian, Corrie Ten Boom, Randy Alcorn, R.T. Kendall, Francis Chan, Gary Smalley, John Trent, Eric Metaxas, Doris Van Stone, Rosaria Champagne Butterfield, and Shirley Elliott.

Carl Zwart – You said I was finding my voice and that I should use it. I hope this book satisfies your welcomed challenge.

Matt and Christie Turnbull – You rock! Thanks for connecting people and for making yourselves deeply available to so many.

Amber McGuire – Our four-hour lunch changed my life. You are an amazing woman. Thank you for praying for me and encouraging me. Rejoicing with you and your steadfast mom for answered prayer!

Debbie Johnson – You are His hands and feet to many. Thanks for encouraging me to write.

Beth Keller – I'm so thankful we are prayer partners and sisters in Christ.

Susan Brockmann – Thanking God for crossing our paths. You are a wonderful blessing.

Aunt Virginia Taylor – a mighty prayer warrior and encourager. You inspire me in so many ways. I love and admire you.

Lin Renberg – I love you and treasure you, my dear sister in Christ and fellow laborer. You are one in a million. Many women know this. I hope we are neighbors in Heaven.

Tracy Howe – I love you, my oldest and trusted friend. I feel your love at all times, but especially at IHOP when you just put your arm around me and said nothing when I poured out my heart. Thank you.

My great son, Nick – You will always be the apple of my eye.

When you were eight, you asked me what I want most, and my answer then is my answer now: to be in Heaven with you so we can enjoy what we've missed in this life – and then some. You have made being your mom such a delight and privilege. You are an amazing young man, and I am so excited to see your beautiful life unfold. The best is yet to be!

My wonderful husband, Daniel – My cheerful companion, attentive confidant, steadfast prayer partner and favorite pilgrim. Your kindness, encouragement and gentleness abounds. Thank you for loving me and laughing with me through thick and thin. I enjoy, love, and respect you. Onward and upward, my Love!

Printed in the United States
By Bookmasters